Windows™ 64-bit Assembly Language Programming Quick Start

Intel® X86-64, SSE, AVX

Robert Dunne

Windows® 64-bit Assembly Language Programming Quick Start: Intel® X86-64, SSE, AVX

Cover Design: Daniel van Loon

ISBN 978-0-970112460 (paperback)

ISBN 978-0-970112453 (digital)

Windows® 64-bit Assembly Language Programming Quick Start: Intel® X86-64, SSE, AVX is an independent publication and has not been authorized, sponsored, or endorsed by any of the hardware or software rights holders described herein.

18 17 16 15 14 13 12 11 10 9 8 7 6 5 4

Contents

Preface

It's time to "Take the bull by the horns" urged my department head as I was stuck in design mode and not moving fast enough into coding. Fortunately, he was referring to a supercomputer interface project I was developing, and not the herd of bison sharing the national laboratory at which we were on staff. Likewise, the purpose of this book is to get students programming in assembly language as quickly as possible without getting too hung up on adjacent topics.

This book is about programming the Intel® X86-64 in assembly language using Microsoft® Visual Studio 17 software. The X86 implies the 16-bit legacy Intel® 8086 processor up through the 64-bit Intel® core i9 and comparable processors from AMD. This is not a book that has been modified or migrates from a 32-bit or 16-bit perspective, but starts right in with 64-bit programming and only refers to past approaches when necessary to explain seemingly unnatural conventions and names.

- All programming examples use the ML64.exe assembler included with the free Community Edition of Microsoft® Visual Studio 17, which is used to develop C and C++ programs running in full 64-bit mode.
- Every sample program is complete, but leaves room for enhancements and experimentation encouraged by the questions at the end of each chapter.
- The sample programs, ranging from five to over one hundred lines of code, are extensively documented in both flow diagrams and comments. All are available for download through GitHub.
- Many assembly language books present CPU instructions in "catalog form" along with snippets of coding examples. In this book, CPU instructions are introduced as needed to achieve programming goals as the projects in each chapter progress to the next.
- Over seventy illustrations are included to explain programming techniques as well as X86, SSE, and AVX instructions.
- Topics like binary and hexadecimal are introduced through programming examples as well as appearing in appendices.
- The examples in this book have been "classroom tested" with students having very little, if any, previous programming experience. The information is complete, allowing it to be used as an independent study.

Audience for This Book

The goal of this book is to assist students and computer enthusiasts get on a solid path to understanding computer architecture and also get a deeper understanding of Microsoft® Windows® programming. The intended audience is the following:

- Anyone wanting to learn assembly language, especially individuals interested in Intel® processors and Microsoft® Windows.
- Someone who already has assembly language experience, but now wants to become familiar with 64-bit programming.

Expected prerequisites for someone reading this book to learn assembly language:

- Access to an Intel® X86-64 based computer running Microsoft® Windows® 7 or 10. This is the norm for desktop and laptop computers sold in the last decade.
- Enough user computer experience to be able to search for files, use a simple editor such as Notepad, and create a directory.
- Internet access to download the free "Community Edition" of Microsoft® Visual Studio if necessary. Many years ago, Microsoft sold its MASM assembler as a separate product, but now its assembler is only available as part of the C++ component of Microsoft® Visual Studio. Many students using this book will have access to computers already loaded with a professional or educational version of Microsoft® Visual Studio. For those who don't, the "Community Edition" is available as a free download from Microsoft, and only the C++ language component is needed.

Why the Microsoft Assembler and Why 64-bit?

There are many assemblers available today, and most are available as a free download. Why study the ML64 assembler in Visual Studio 17 instead of others?

- ML64 works both in a traditional Command Line Interface approach and in an Integrated Development Environment (IDE), including its editor and powerful interactive debugger.
- Assembly Language programming in 64-bit mode is much easier than in 16-bit mode or in 32-bit mode. The horrific memory management techniques using segment registers to squeeze applications into small memory spaces are no longer needed. The variety and inconsistency of subroutine calling "conventions" of 32-bit applications have been

simplified in 64-bit Windows.

- Microsoft® Windows® 10 will not run 16-bit applications. Even 32-bit applications cannot run directly, but must be partially run in an emulation mode. Some day they may be eliminated as well.
- The ML64 assembler is free and down-loadable from Microsoft.

Book Organization

How can a 200 page book be a "quick start"? Basically, you only have to go as far as you want. Either Chapter 2 or Chapter 13 is enough to get a person programming and running 64-bit assembly language programs using Microsoft® Visual Studio.

- The first chapter introduces the concept and structure of CPU "machine code" in general using examples modeled as a calculator. Those already familiar with CPU architectures in general can easily skip this chapter.
- Chapter 2 provides a command line work flow for developing all of the test programs in the remainder of this book. It includes directions on locating the ML64 assembler, linker, and library, as well as setting up working directories for writing test programs.
- Chapter 3 introduces Windows function calls with a program that reads from the keyboard and writes to the monitor. This read/write console program is then gradually enhanced in Chapters 4 and 5 with additional assembly language instructions and programming techniques using macros, subroutines, and nested loops.
- Chapter 6 focuses on the linker and divides the console application into multiple source files, object files, and a link library.
- In Chapters 7 and 8, more subroutines are added to the console program to produce ASCII, binary, decimal, and hexadecimal outputs showcasing several more instructions.
- Chapter 9 begins a new console program focusing on memory addressing schemes and string instructions.
- Chapters 10, 11, and 12 focus on SIMD (Single Instruction Multiple Data) programming including the SSE and AVX enhancements and floating point.
- Chapter 13 details the set up of the C++ IDE in 64-bit mode and has examples of a C program combined with assembly language as well as a program totally in assembly language. This chapter highlights the powerful interactive debugger and provides further examples implementing the X64 Calling Convention.
- Eight appendices present background information on setting up Visual Studio, batch command processing, binary, hexadecimal, Windows function calls, and summaries of X86-64 instructions and assembler directives used in this book.

IDE or Command Line Interface?

With Microsoft® Visual Studio 17, assembly language programs can be built using either its Integrated Development Environment (IDE) or using the ML64 assembler directly in a traditional command line approach. Both techniques are presented in this book, and each has its own merits for gaining a deeper understanding of computer software and hardware.

The Visual Studio 17 IDE combines a text editor, file organizer, compilers, linker, and an interactive debugger in a single package that is fairly easy to use. However, it "hides" much of what it is doing to generate a working program.

Beginning with Chapter 2, this book uses the command line approach to introduce X86-64 instructions, programming techniques, and program linking and libraries. It ends with Chapter 13 that uses the IDE to build applications containing both C and assembly language, as well as 100% assembly language programs. For those who like to start from the end and work to the beginning, Chapter 13 does show how to produce a 64-bit 100% assembly language program using the IDE. One could then use the IDE's editor and interactive debugger for chapters 2 through 12.

I recommend readers make two passes through this book: 1) Use command line mode to get familiar with the registers, instructions, assembling, and linking, and 2) Use the interactive debugger to monitor registers, flags, and memory locations as each program progresses. No matter which approach you prefer, it is now time to "Take the bull by the horns" and get down to coding.

About the Author

Robert Dunne has over 40 years of computer experience ranging from developing custom hardware interfaces on supercomputers to teaching technology courses in middle-school gifted-education programs. Starting out with degrees in physics and computer science, he was on staff at a national laboratory and a major engineering firm for ten years before becoming an entrepreneur in the development of embedded systems. He has written well over 100,000 lines of assembler code developing systems and applications on ten unique CPU architectures encompassing mainframes, minicomputers, and microcomputers.

During the past twelve years, he has taught three undergraduate courses per semester in digital electronics and embedded systems and is notorious for getting his students working on a lab project within the first 60 seconds of the very first class meeting.

— 1 —
The Calculator

When I ask my students when do they think the first computers were developed, I usually get answers like the 1980s or even the 1940s. Very few know that the basic architecture of almost all computers used in the past 50 years dates back to the 1830s with Charles Babbage's Analytical Engine.

Figure 1.1: Babbage's Analytical Engine

Babbage's Analytical Engine consisted of two principal components:

- Mill: The hardware that did the work (arithmetic and logic operations)
- Store: Location for data storage of intermediate results

Figure 1.2: "Modern" computer hardware nomenclature

Babbage's mill and store correspond to today's computers:

- CPU (Central Processing Unit): The hardware that does the work (arithmetic and logic operations)
- Memory: Location for data storage of intermediate results

By no means am I implying there existed a positive progression of concepts and devices from Babbage's day to today. The computer pioneers in the 1940s recreated much of what was lost for nearly one hundred years. I personally observed the microcomputer software industry in the 1980s recreate the same mistakes and going down the same wrong paths as the mainframe developers did in the 1960s.

The Machine and Its Language

"Machine Language" generally refers to the numeric codes that instruct the CPU what operation is to be performed and on what values.

Figure 1.3: Simple calculator model

In order to understand machine language, think of a calculator which has the following features:

- **Display:** Current number being entered or current result of operations
- **Operations:** Clear (C), add(+), subtract(-), multiply(*), divide(/), display(=)
- **Data input:** Digits and decimal point, sign(+/-), clear entry (CE), back space (BS)

When we use a simple calculator, there is a symbiotic partnership to achieve the final calculation: The calculator does the work, and we provide the directions.

We enter the following sequence of instructions to perform the calculation 13×21+6:

1. **Clear**
2. **Add 13**
3. **Multiply 21**
4. **Add 6**
5. **Display**

Registers

CPUs contain a small number of fast-access memory locations called registers. Depending upon the particular CPU design, the number of registers varies from about five up to nearly one hundred. Some of the registers are accessible to user programs in assembly language, and some registers are only accessed by the CPU's electronics to perform its many tasks. The principal data register is generally referred to as the "accumulator." In our calculator example, the accumulator value is that "running total" or accumulated total that is in the display.

Most of the logical and arithmetic operations performed by CPUs are binary operations. Two numbers (called operands) are added, or two operands are multiplied, or one operand is subtracted from another. In our calculator example, the first operand is the value in the display (i.e., the accumulator), and the second operand is the number being entered.

Op-codes

Although a CPU could be constructed to work with the character string names of operations like clear, add, and multiply, it would be somewhat inefficient. Instead, the CPU designers assign a numeric operation code (op-code) to represent each of the available CPU operations. For example, let the following six numbers be assigned to the following six calculator operations:

1. **Clear (C)**: Load zero into the accumulator.
2. **Add (+)**: Add the value of the operand (being entered) to the current accumulator contents.
3. **Subtract (-)**: Subtract the value of the operand (being entered) from the current accumulator contents.
4. **Multiply (*)**: Multiply the value of the operand (being entered) to the current accumulator contents.
5. **Divide (/)**: Divide the current contents of the accumulator by the operand (being entered).
6. **Display (=)**: Copy the current contents of the accumulator to the display line.

If we use the above numeric assignments to translate our previous sequence of instructions to calculate $13\times21+6$, we will get the following machine code:

Step number	Operation		Op-code with operand
1	Clear	translates to	1 : 0
2	Add 13	translates to	2 : 13
3	Multiply 21	translates to	4 : 21
4	Add 6	translates to	2 : 6
5	Display	translates to	6 : 0

Table 1.1: Translate "assembly code" into "machine code."

Note that in this simple model of a calculator being used as a computer, I've represented each instruction as a binomial: an op-code and operand pair. In Table 1.1's translation to machine code, binary operations like Add and Multiply are converted to form "op-code : operand" pairs. Unitary operations, such as Clear and Display, are converted to the form "op-code : 0" because there was no operand. So in this example, we would calculate 13×21+6 by entering "Clear, Add 13, Multiply 21, Add 6, Display" on a calculator, but the corresponding computer program (in machine language) would be the sequence "1 : 0, 2 : 13, 4 : 21, 2 : 6, 6 : 0."

Memory

What about the other half of Babbage's computer: the "store" ("memory" in today's terminology)? Babbage needed memory for the storage of intermediate results and so do we. In an arithmetic problem like 13×14+15×16, we can't just multiply 13 times 14, add 15, and then multiply by 16. The answer would be wrong because by convention, multiplication has precedence over addition: the 15 and 16 have to be multiplied before being added to the product of 13 and 14. There is an implied parenthesis in this calculation as follows: (13×14)+(15×16). With our non-memory calculator, we would have to write down the intermediate value of 13×14 and then reenter it after we calculate 15×16. Memory calculators do this "writing down" and reentering for us.

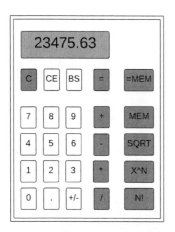

Figure 1.4: Memory Calculator with functions

In our calculator model shown in Figure 1.4, we have more operations, two of which are related to memory: Store (=MEM) and Load (MEM). Since we added two more operations to the calculator, we must also add two more op-codes: Store (op-code = 7) and Load (op-code = 8).

Op-codes 1 through 8 are defined as follows:

1. **Clear (C)**
2. **Add (+)**
3. **Subtract (-)**
4. **Multiply (*)**
5. **Divide (/)**

6. **Display (=)**
7. **Store (=MEM)**: Copy the contents of the accumulator into a memory location.
8. **Load (MEM)**: Copy the contents of a memory location into the accumulator.

Is this the best approach for using memory? The above Store command is fine, but the Load instruction is too limiting. In some simple memory calculators that store only one value in memory, there is an "Add memory" command, but what if you want to multiply using the value in memory or divide by it? What we really would like is to not just reload a saved value, but use it in any of the previously defined operations such as Add or Multiply.

Most CPU implementations include a "flag" in the instruction that indicates if the operand is immediate (value in the operand) or is from memory. Our binomial instruction format (op-code and operand) now becomes a trinomial (op-code, immediate-flag, and operand). If we use the above operations including the new immediate flag to write a little program to calculate $13 \times 14 + 15 \times 16$, we will get the following code:

Step number	Operation		Op-code :i- flag : operand
1	Clear	translates to	$1:1:0$
2	Add 13	translates to	$2:1:13$
3	Multiply 14	translates to	$4:1:14$
4	Store Mem 0	translates to	$7:0:0$
5	Clear	translates to	$1:1:0$
6	Add 15	translates to	$2:1:15$
7	Multiply 16	translates to	$4:1:16$
8	Add Mem 0	translates to	$2:0:0$
9	Display	translates to	$6:1:0$

Table 1.2: Translate "assembly code" into "machine code."

The above system actually works fine, but can we improve on the performance? Storing intermediate results into memory always takes time. An accumulator is also memory, but it's very fast local memory inside the CPU, and we can also use it as an operand in our instructions. Although some CPUs have only one accumulator, the vast majority have several. The X86-64 architecture has 16 user accessible general purpose registers, most of which can be used as accumulators for making calculations.

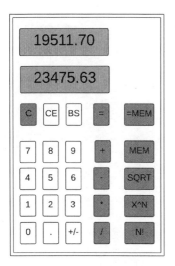

Figure 1.5: Two-accumulator Calculator

Let's expand our calculator model to have two accumulators and see how that changes our assembly language. First, our instructions are no longer trinomials consisting of three numbers, but now have a fourth component: we have to specify which accumulator is being used in the operation. In the previous one-accumulator calculator model, we only had one accumulator, so it was the only one that could be used and therefore did not need to be specified.

Step number	Operation		Op-code : acc : i-flag : operand
1	Clear A0	translates to	1 : 0 : 1 : 0
2	Add 13 to A0	translates to	2 : 0 : 1 : 13
3	Multiply A0 by 14	translates to	4 : 0 : 1 : 14
4	Clear A1	translates to	1 : 1 : 1 : 0
5	Add 15 to A1	translates to	2 : 1 : 1 : 15
6	Multiply A1 by 16	translates to	4 : 1 : 1 : 16
7	Add A1 to A0	translates to	2 : 0 : 0 : 1
8	Display A0	translates to	6 : 0 : 1 : 0

Table 1.3: Use two accumulators: A0 and A1

Any Other Instructions?

Computers are great for doing the same thing over and over again, but on different sets of input data. Sometimes, we write a program to perform the calculations differently, depending on the type and values of the data being processed. Making these decisions, as well as knowing when to exit these repetitive loops are done by jump instructions (a.k.a., branch instructions) and conditional test instructions. We'll examine these techniques in the next section on documentation, but we'll not implement them here in this calculator model.

Language Interpreter and Compiler

The "human language" source code of our programs must be translated to machine language in order to be executed by the CPU. This translation can be done all at once before any of the machine code is executed or it can be converted and executed line by line as it is needed. The two approaches are the following:

- Interpreter: Translate each line of source code to machine language line by line just before it is executed.
- Compiler: Convert the entire source code file to machine language all at one time.

Assembly language as well as C and Java are almost always compiled. Languages like Basic have traditionally been interpreted. There are merits to each approach which we won't go into here except saying that interpreter code is easier to write and debug, while compiled code offers much higher performance at execution time.

As in most things, there's always a slight modification in order. Java and Microsoft's .net programming languages like VB.net and C# don't compile all the way to machine language. They compile to an intermediate language that is very close to a generic machine language, not tied to any particular CPU.

Assembly Language

A machine language instruction is composed of multiple integer fields indicating which operation is to be performed and on what data. Assembly language substitutes names for these integers, and generates one machine code instruction for each line of assembly language coding. Almost every assembly language program for all CPUs consists of four columns:

1. Label: Name associated with instruction's memory address
2. Op-code: The operation being performed (add, sub, shift, ...)
3. Operands: Location of the data (usually a register combined with a constant, another register, or memory address)
4. Comment: Describes why the instruction is being used

nxtlin:	mov	RCX,stdout	; Handle to standard output device
	lea	RDX,msg	; Pointer to prompt message
	mov	R8,lengthof msg	; Number of characters to display
	lea	R9,nbwr	; Number of bytes actually written.
	call	WriteConsoleA	; Write text string to command box.

Listing 1.1: Example of assembly language source code

Each column is separated by one or more blanks or tab characters. How wide is a column? Typical columns are 8 to 10 characters wide with the exception of the rightmost column which contains comments. The assembler doesn't care if it's one blank, two blanks, or more that separates the data from one column to the next. We line up the columns of assembly code for the ease of reading by the programmers.

Comments

There is more to a well-written program than the machine code itself. Program design and maintenance requires documentation. "Internal documentation" is the description of the program appearing in the program itself and consists of two types of comments:

1. **Global**: These comments describe what a section of code is doing. They normally consist of more than one line of text and are not on the same physical text lines as the actual machine code instructions. Global comments are used in both assembly language as well as higher level languages.
2. **Local**: These comments share the text line with the actual machine code instructions. They are rarely needed in higher level languages, but are very important in assembly language to explain not what the code is doing but *why* the line of code is doing it.

Importance of comments: They're not necessary for a program to successfully run, and many programmers use very few comments. They're necessary for program maintenance, whether it be by a new programmer next week or by the original programmer a month or even several years later. When I was an undergraduate student and took a course in assembly language programming, my professor thought comments were so important that he subtracted one letter grade for each line of code that didn't have a local comment. That was a bit extreme, but I got the point. I confess that in my production code I don't comment every line, but I do comment much more than others. In this book, I will be commenting on almost every line to help set an example as well as explain what's going on in the code.

The following excerpt from an assembly language program shows both global (first two lines) and local comments. There are almost as many ways to mark the beginning of a comment as there are programming languages. In this book, I will be using the semicolon, which is the most popular character in assembly language to indicate the beginning of a comment. In other assemblers, the comment indicator is #, /, . (period) or @ (at-sign). In other computer languages, comments are indicated by <!, /* with */, //, - -, #, C, and even REM.

```
;          Macro "msgOut msg" displays a character string in command window.
;                    msg:   Label of ASCII message for command window.

msgOut    macro    msg                 ; One argument: msg
          mov      RCX,stdout          ; Handle to standard output device
          lea      RDX,msg             ; Pointer to message to display
          mov      R8,lengthof  msg    ; Number of characters to display
          lea      R9,nbwr             ; Number of bytes actually written.
          call     WriteConsoleA       ; Write text to command window.
          endm
```

Listing 1.2: Sample of local and global comments

Documentation

Program documentation is used during both construction and long term operation of a software application. It tells the development programmers what the application is supposed to do and tells maintenance programmers what the application is doing and how it's doing it.

Some computer languages are somewhat self-documenting. Assembly language is definitely not one of these. One of the first languages developed after assembly language was Cobol which has been present in business applications for over 50 years. Although professionally trained programmers were needed to write Cobol programs, almost anyone who could read English could read the Cobol program instructions and get a very good understanding of what was being done. Even today's commonly used languages like C and Java contain structures like loops and objects which help identify what is being done in the program.

Documentation basically exists at three levels:

1. **Narrative**: A description in words, charts, tables, and examples explaining what the application does. To some degree it even recommends how the application should perform its assigned tasks.
2. **Diagrams**: There has been a variety of graphic modeling languages over the years beginning with traditional flowcharts through the Universal Modeling Language (UML). Their diagrams show program structure and flow.
3. **Internal documentation in the code itself**: All programs should have comments interspersed among lines of code saying what is being done, why it's being done, and how it's being done. For higher level languages like C and Java, internal documentation is important. In assembly language it is crucial.

I never really liked flowcharts. However, many students new to programming say this graphical approach helps them grasp the logic flow more readily. So I'll use them in the first few chapters to explain some programming techniques and even use them to explain how a machine code instruction works.

I'll be using three basic flowchart symbols (and then three alterations to one of them).

- **Process**: Identifies a task, such as adding three numbers.
- **Decision**: Shows alternate paths the program can take based upon current values in the data.
- **Terminator**: Identifies the beginning and ending points of a portion of the program

Figure 1.7: Basic flowchart symbols

Although I could use the process block throughout, I will also use three other symbols when the process is more specific: preparation, predefined process, and display.

- **Preparation**: A process like initializing a running total to zero (i.e., it is a process, but not the "main act")
- **Predefined Process**: A compound process like taking the square root (normally located external to the current program coding)
- **Display**: A process where the computer user receives a displayed message.

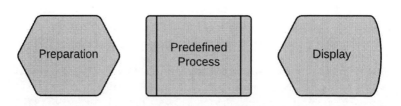

Figure 1.8: Specialized process symbols

Figure 1.9 provides a flowchart example of a procedure that calculates the sum of a series of numbers using a calculator. After turning on the calculator and pushing clear, a series of numbers are entered from the keypad. This is actually a multi-step procedure where one or more numeric keys are pushed and may include a decimal point. See Figure 1.10 for the "sub" routine that will "Enter Number from Keypad."

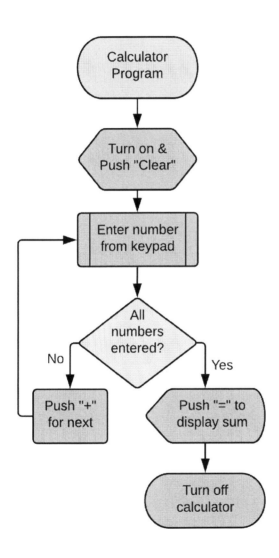

Figure 1.9: Program using predefined process

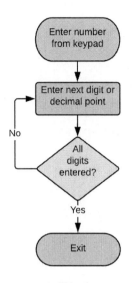

Figure 1.10 illustrates the "predefined process" of "Enter number from keypad" called from the previous flowchart. Predefined processes, also known as subroutines, procedures, functions, and methods, are common to computer programming languages. Their use provides a structure leading to more reliable as well as more compact code. Most of the programming examples in this book involve building subroutines to perform specific tasks.

Figure 1.10: Predefined process
"Enter number from keyboard"

Figure 1.11: Connecting
segments of a flowchart

The final flowchart symbol that appears for very large programs is the off-page link. It is used to divide a single flowchart into smaller segments. With a large piece of paper, off-page links would neither be necessary nor used very often. It will not be necessary to use that symbol in this book due to the size of program segments that are being discussed.

The Universal Modeling Language (UML) has been available for many years for documenting software structure (usually for higher level languages) and development on many levels. Its "activity diagram" is the closest thing to traditional flowcharts, and it has some added real-time (i.e., embedded systems) features. Also, pseudo code which uses a somewhat arbitrary program-like verbal description of how the code works is more popular today.

Numbers

Both integers and real numbers are used in applications software. They reside in computer registers and memory in binary and floating point formats, respectively. Integers are also used for memory addresses of program instructions and data. The following number formats are present in assembly language:

- Decimal: Base 10, having digits 0 through 9, is used to represent most numbers used in arithmetic calculations.
- Binary: Integers contained in registers and memory are stored as a group of binary digits (bits), zeroes and ones. The sizes of the "containers" range from an 8-bit byte to a 64-bit "quad word." Please see Appendix G for more information on binary format.
- Hexadecimal: Hexadecimal is base 16 and is found in assembly language programs because it's a compact way to represent binary. Appendix H has more information on hexadecimal format.
- Scientific Notation: Very small and very large numbers used in science and engineering are represented in computers in floating point format, which is very similar to scientific notation. Please see Chapter 12 for more information on floating point format.
- Negative: Negative numbers in decimal are preceded by the minus sign. All floating point numbers can be positive or negative, but integers can be either signed or unsigned (i.e., whole numbers). Appendix G has further details.

A variable in algebra is a symbol or name that represents or "stands in" for a number. Likewise, most assemblers support variables that can be assigned numeric values, and they fall into three categories:

- Run-time data variables: Data being processed by an application program are stored in memory at specific addresses. Although these addresses could be entered as integers, associating a name with them is much more convenient.
- Assembly-time variables: Assembly language provides a flexible scheme to represent constants that do not change during the running of a program, but programmers might want to change them when the program is altered for improvements. The size of a table is an example of a fixed value that might be increased on decreased when the program design is altered.
- Program addresses: Addresses of machine code instructions are integers, some being absolute and others being relative to a particular location.

Review Questions

1. What advantage does a second accumulator give a CPU? What's the disadvantage?
2. Most CPU instructions use two operands. If one operand is a register, what can the second operand be?
3. How are a compiler and an interpreter similar? How are they different?
4. * "By hand, without a calculator or computer," convert the following numbers expressed in decimal to binary format. See Appendix G if you need some background in binary.
   - a. 21
   - b. 63
   - c. 16
   - d. 129
   - e. 13
5. * "By hand, without a calculator or computer," convert the following numbers expressed in binary to decimal format. See Appendix G if you need some background in binary.
   - a. 1011
   - b. 1100101
   - c. 10110
   - d. 100001
   - e. 1111011
6. Draw a flowchart for eating a bowl of soup. To start with, it should contain a process: "Dip spoon into soup" as well as a decision: "Is the bowl empty?" Other components will of course be necessary to complete the flowchart.

Programming Exercises

1. Write an assembly language program to calculate: 45×16÷7-46. Note: I'm not talking about using the real X86-64 instructions, but the simple ones made up for the calculator example (like the example in Table 1.1).
2. Hand assemble your "program" (from Exercise 1). That is, convert the op-code mnemonics to their numeric values (like the example in Table 1.1).
3. Write an assembly language program for the memory calculator to generate: 31+45×37 (like the example in Table 1.2).
4. Rewrite the above exercise using the two-accumulator calculator without using memory locations.

— 2 —
Compile, Link, Execute

From a programmer's perspective, software development is a vicious cycle of modify the program, test the program, modify the program, test the program, modify the program, test the program until we are satisfied with the test results. As described in Chapter 1, an assembly language program consists of lines of text which we create and modify using a simple text editor. We then test the program by translating it into X86-64 machine code to be run in a command console window. In this book, we use the ML64 assembler and its associated linker included with Microsoft Visual Studio 2017.

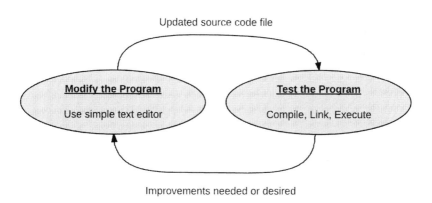

Figure 2.1: Program development and testing

Simple First Program

Let's begin the vicious software development cycle with a simple program that starts and then exits. We will need to create a working directory, use the Notepad editor to write the source code file, run the ML64 assembler, link to the Windows 64-bit Application Programming Interface (API) library, run the created program, and display its exit status. Once set up here, the same compile-link-execute procedure will be easily performed in all of the following chapters.

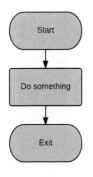

Figure 2.2: Program flow

The flowchart in figure 2.2 illustrates the major flow of a program: It gets CPU control, it does its intended job, and finally it returns control.

The only purpose of this first program (Listing 2.1) is to start and then quit. How does a computer start, run, and stop? The hardware knows where to start the first instruction after power-up or reset, and there is an X86 instruction that effectively halts its execution. Those instructions are controlled by the Windows operating system in the environment in which we're working.

```
1.                includelib    kernel32.lib
2. ExitProcess    proto
3.                .code
4. main           proc                        ; Program external name
5.                mov           RCX,78         ; Load exit status code into RCX
6.                call          ExitProcess    ; Return CPU control to Windows
7. main           endp
8.                end
```

Listing 2.1: First program: C:\ASM64\main.asm

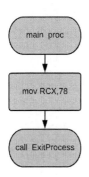

Figure 2.3: Windows X86-64

A program starts when Windows gives it control at its "ENTRY" point; and when your program chooses to quit, it will return control back to Windows using the "ExitProcess" function call. Actually, Windows never gives up full control to your program, but don't be concerned about that for now.

Windows provides a variety of services to a running program such as reading and writing disk files, and communicating with keyboards, monitors, and networks. When an application terminates, it returns an "exit code" in register RCX to Windows that can be tested in command line scripts, or simply displayed by the "echo %errorlevel%" command line.

Introductions

Each chapter in this book has an **Introductions** section describing X86-64 CPU instructions not seen in previous chapters. Most chapters will also introduce ML64 assembler directives that clarify and simplify how the source code is to be converted into a running program by the assembler and linker. All eight lines of Listing 2.1 are described below (It is the first program and everything is new).

1. INCLUDELIB: Identify external library, such as kernel32.lib that contains linkages to the Windows Application Programming Interface (API). Note: Even though the file name says "32," this library file contains the 64-bit Windows functions.
2. PROTO: The prototype directive informs the assembler of the name of an external function (a.k.a., procedure) that will be called. ExitProcess will be called on line 6.
3. .CODE: Just like Babbage's computer had the mill and store, today's computers have code (instructions) and data areas. Note: The .CODE directive begins with a period. The .CODE directive marks the beginning of a section containing X86-64 instructions, while the .DATA directive (introduced in the next chapter) marks the beginning of a data section in memory.
4. PROC: Programs are divided into procedures and each is given a name. The name "main" is arbitrary, but is commonly used to name the principle component of a program. Whatever you choose, and I recommend you continue to use main, it must match the name on the ENTRY option to the linker.
5. MOV: This is the first actual X86-64 machine code instruction in the program, and here it simply loads a decimal 78 into the 64-bit RCX register. Two more instructions, ADD and SUB, will be used in the next program in this chapter.
6. CALL: This CALL machine code instruction will jump to the Windows ExitProcess function, and thereby return full control of the CPU back to Windows.
7. ENDP: Every procedure has a beginning and an end. This ENDP directive marks the end of the "main" procedure code.
8. END: Every assembler source text file has a beginning and an end, so the END directive marks the end of this simple program.

Is assembly language case sensitive? In other words, is "INCLUDELIB" different from "includelib"? In general, case does not matter in assembly language. It's primarily your choice and style. From what I've observed, the majority of programmers use lowercase for programming. In this book's program listings, I will provide the register names in uppercase and everything else generally in lower case. I will note exceptions where case is critical.

Program User Interface

Almost every operating system today supports programs that provide the following user interfaces:

- Graphical User Interface (GUI), (Windows Desktop Application): This is the most popular interface today, where the user inputs data through a combination of mouse movements, clicks, and keyboard input.
- Command Line Interface, (Windows Console Application): This mode can be traced back to the early mainframe days when input was on punched cards and output on continuous forms paper. The ML64 assembler is a command line program, and so is the "visual" C++ compiler for that matter.

The following five steps of the software development and testing cycle are illustrated in Figure 2.4:

1. **Edit (make the source code):** The source code such as that shown in Listing 2.1 has to be entered (or copied) into a text file.
2. **Compile (make the object code):** Each "machine language" instruction executed by the X86-64 CPU is composed of several fields ("groups of bits"), which could be entered as integers, but would be a lot of work. In assembly language, the fields are entered with mnemonic names and decimal, hexadecimal, or binary numbers. The ML64 assembler program converts the text lines to the binary instructions (object code).
3. **Link (make the executable program):** The LINK (linker) program combines multiple object files into a single executable file.
4. **Execute (run the program):** This step is the objective of the previous three steps, but how do you know if your program is doing what you wanted it to do or is even doing anything at all? You'll need some type of I/O (Input/Output).
5. **Examine results:** In this chapter, we'll use the echo command line to assist with a little output using the value of the exit status in register RCX. Chapter 3 will demonstrate input from the keyboard and output to the monitor screen.

File names appearing in Figure 2.4:

- **main.asm:** Source file containing assembly language text
- **main.obj:** Object file containing X86-64 machine code
- **main.exe:** Executable file ready to run on 64-bit Windows computer.

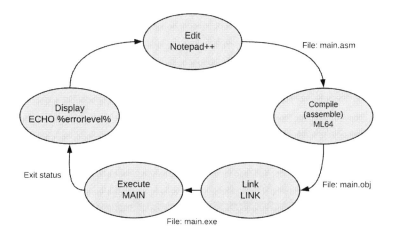

Figure 2.4: Work flow of testing a program update

Set Up Working Environment

The following steps are needed to set up the working environment that will be used for developing and testing programs in command line mode.

1. Create a directory: Program development involves files: source code, object code, and executable "machine code" files. In the examples, I put all of these files in one directory named "C:\ASM64," but a directory name of your own choosing will also be fine.

2. Find the KERNEL32.LIB library file: The Application Programming Interface (API) to the 64-bit operating system functions is contained in a file, oddly enough named KERNEL32.LIB. Note: There are many libraries with the same file name, but the others are for 32-bit applications or the ARM processor. You should copy the correct file to your working directory (C:\ASM64 in my examples).

3. Find the ML64 assembler: It is quite likely that your computer already has the ML64 assembler present. If not, the C++ compiler of Microsoft® Visual Studio® will need to be downloaded and installed. A "path" will then need to be created to the directory containing ML64 and the associated LINK program.

4. Download sample programs: All of the assembly programs shown in this book are available as a free download from GitHub. It is, of course, possible to key in all the examples, but who really wants to do that? It is also possible to get a good idea how to program in assembly language simply by reading this book and not running any of the examples, but most people think hands-on practice is more effective.

Create ASM64 Directory

Create a directory to hold the source code, object code, and executable "machine code" files. Since I use a directory named "C:\ASM64" in the examples, I recommend you also create a directory named ASM64, so it matches the examples, but any directory will be fine. The examples will still work.

The first program in Listing 2.1 can now be entered into a text file named main.asm.

1. What text editor to use? Notepad is available on all Windows computers and will work fine. I prefer Notepad++ which is a free download from notepad-plus-plus.org and provides extra features like displaying line numbers. Word processing programs cannot be used because they include text formatting commands, such as font changes and underlining in the files they create.
2. Are the line numbers entered? No. The line numbers are for us humans only, and the assembler does not want line numbers in the file. Notepad++ can show line numbers while Notepad does not.
3. How many blanks are between columns? One or more. The assembler does not care. I use the tab to separate columns so it is easier to have the text lining up properly. The straight columns are for us humans, not the assembler.
4. Does the file name have to be "main.asm"? No, it could even be X.1, but I'll be using main.asm in the examples, and this really is the "main" "assembly" program being used in this book. In the long run, it is best to be consistent with the "asm" file type convention. Remember: In Notepad, you must "Save as Type" "All Files," or else the file type will default to TXT.

An alternative approach is to use the Visual Studio IDE which has a built-in editor, file organizer and interactive debugger. I recommend making a second pass through all the program examples in this book after setting up the IDE for 64-bit assembly language programs as shown in Chapter 13.

Copy the KERNEL32.LIB File

In Listing 2.1 line 6, the main.asm program calls the Windows ExitProcess function. This function and many others, such as those that read and write files and devices, are contained in a library file named kernel32.lib. Your computer probably has several versions of the kernel32.lib file: one for 32-bit applications, one for 64-bit applications, as well as versions for other processors like the ARM.

Open up Windows "File Explorer" as seen in Figure 2.5, set the base directory to C:\ and file name to kernel32.lib, push the Enter key and wait for the search results.

Figure 2.5: Search results for KERNEL32.LIB

Move the mouse to hover over each of the kernel32.lib files, looking for one ending in X64 as show in Figure 2.6. Right click on this one and copy it into the C:\ASM64 directory you just created. Be sure to copy, not "move," because you don't want to remove kernel32.lib from where it is already located.

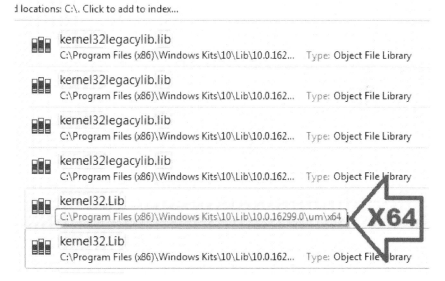

Figure 2.6: Zoom in of Figure 2.5 to identify desired KERNEL32.LIB

In the event you cannot find any kernel32.lib files or the X64 one in particular, then you currently don't have a 64-bit version of Visual Studio installed on your computer, or it is installed on a different disk drive than C. Appendix A provides advice on how to download the free Community Edition of Visual Studio 2017. You will only need the C++ compiler portion, not the entire package. Once loaded, you can perform the above search again.

Open the CMD Window

Because ML64 is a console program and we want to focus on assembly language at this time, we will use the "Windows Command Processor" (CMD window) for compiling and testing rather than the Visual Studio IDE (Integrated Development Environment). The easiest way to start this command window is to enter CMD followed by the Enter key in the "search" box on the Windows taskbar. The following three commands should then be entered in the command window to arrive at the desired working directory.

- C:
- CD \ASM64
- DIR

Only the CD (Change Directory) command should be needed, but the other two commands won't hurt to be included. The first line should not be needed because the CMD processor will usually default to your C directory. The third line produces a directory which should show both the KERNEL32.LIB file and the MAIN.ASM file that you just entered. Of course, these commands can be entered in lower case as well. For more information on the command processor, please see Appendix B.

Path command

If you enter ML64 in the command window to start the assembler, you will probably get the following error response:

> 'ML64' is not recognized as an internal or external command, operable program or batch file.

The assembler and linker are not special Windows CMD processor commands, but console programs just like the ones we will be building. The CMD processor must be told where they are located, so we must first find them, and then set a "path" to them.

Use a similar search as you did in Figure 2.5, but the file name is ML64.EXE instead of KERNEL32.LIB. You could, of course, copy both the ML64.EXE and LINK.EXE program files to C:\ASM64 as you did for the KERNEL32.LIB file, but a better way is to set a path to the directory containing both the assembler and linker.

path C:\######\Hostx64\x64;%PATH%

The above path statement consists of the word "path" followed by the file location containing the ML64 assembler, followed by a semicolon, and finally %PATH%. The file location will vary from computer to computer (that's why we searched for it), but it will probably begin with "C:\Program Files (x86)\Microsoft Visual Studio" and end with "\Hostx64\x64" (I have shown the middle as a series of # hash tags). The semicolon followed by %PATH% enables the new path to be included with any previous paths, but not replace them.

Listing 2.2 shows the path command and assembler both being entered in the command window. On the assembler command, I have used the /c option so that the main.asm program will only be assembled, not linked in this example. Note that this is a lower case c. Appendix B provides a description of the ML64 command line and its options. We will normally not be just assembling in the future, but linking as well.

You have probably noticed that some things are case sensitive and some things are not. Just like in program source code, programmers commonly use lower case for commands. I will be starting the assembler as ML64 because the lower case ml64 looks too much like "m" followed by the number 164.

```
C:\ASM64> path C:\######\Hostx64\x64;%PATH%
C:\ASM64>ML64 /c main.asm
Microsoft (R) Macro Assembler (x64) Version 14.11.25547.0
Copyright (C) Microsoft Corporation. All rights reserved.

Assembling: main.asm

C:\ASM64>
```

Listing 2.2: Path command with assembly of main.asm program

The path statement is rather long and has to be entered whenever the CMD processor is started. You might want to put it into a batch file named something like setpath.bat and simply enter setpath instead. Don't name the batch file path.bat, or else you will have trouble getting to the real path command. Appendix B describes batch file commands in more detail.

Once started and after entering the path command, you will probably leave the command window open for several iterations of compile-link-execute. Before closing down your computer, you should close the command window by either entering the EXIT command or simply "X"ing out with a mouse click.

Compile, Link, and Run First Program

Since the MAIN.ASM file is now present, let's continue the vicious software development cycle by assembling, linking, running, and checking status with the following three commands in the command window.

    1. ML64 main.asm /link /SUBSYSTEM:CONSOLE /ENTRY:main
    2. main
    3. echo %errorlevel%

The first line calls in the ML64 assembler with the following file name and options:

- main.asm => Since only one file name is entered, main.asm is assumed to contain the assembly source program. The object file generated will be main.obj.
- /link => If the assembly is good, then also call in the linker to make an executable file which will be named main.exe. Note: "/link" must be lower case, not /LINK.
- /SUBSYSTEM:CONSOLE => A console program is to be created for CMD mode execution. This is actually a command to the linker.
- /ENTRY:main => The program will start with a procedure named "main." Note: This parameter is case sensitive (MAIN and Main do not match the name main in the source code). This is also a command for the linker.

Please see Appendix B for an explanation of additional assembler command line options. The second command line ("main") starts the main.exe program. The "echo %errorlevel%" command line displays the exit status from running the main.exe program.

```
C:\ASM64>ML64 main.asm /link /SUBSYSTEM:CONSOLE /ENTRY:main
Microsoft (R) Macro Assembler (x64) Version 14.11.25547.0
Copyright (C) Microsoft Corporation. All rights reserved.

Assembling: main.asm
Microsoft (R) Incremental Linker Version 14.11.25547.0
Copyright (C) Microsoft Corporation. All rights reserved.

/OUT:main.exe
main.obj
/SUBSYSTEM:CONSOLE
/ENTRY:main

C:\ASM64>main
```

```
C:\ASM64>echo %errorlevel%
78

C:\ASM64>
```

Listing 2.3: Windows CMD commands to compile, link, and execute

Listing 2.3 shows the CMD window display from entering the ML64, main, and echo commands. Notice in particular that there is no output from executing the main program, but the echo command does provide the value "78" from the exit status value. Figure 2.7 illustrates the above by showing three open windows: file explorer, CMD window, and Notepad.

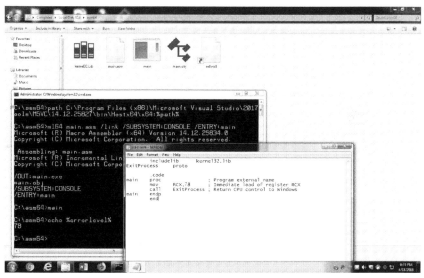

Figure 2.7: Three windows open: File explorer, CMD, and Notepad

Addition and Subtraction

Let's make the example a little more interesting by including some computation. The following lines of code will be inserted into the main program to include addition and subtraction. Each instruction has its first operand being a 64-bit register, and the second operand is either an immediate constant or another register. Only one output will still be displayed (the exit status) by the echo command.

- mov   RCX, 1
- add   RCX, 100
- mov   RDX, 10
- sub   RCX, RDX

1.	includelib	kernel32.lib	
2. ExitProcess	proto		
3.	.code		
4. main	proc		; Program external name
5.	mov	RCX,1	; Immediate load of register RCX
6.	add	RCX,100	; Immediate add to contents of RCX
7.	mov	RDX,10	; Register RDX loaded with decimal 10
8.	sub	RCX,RDX	; Subtract register RDX from RCX
9.	call	ExitProcess	; Return CPU control to Windows
10. main	endp		
11.	end		

Listing 2.4: A simple "calculation" of 1 + 100 - 10.

Go ahead and run the updated program. The "answer" output from the echo command will be 91, of course. Try some other combinations to get accustomed to the edit-compile-link-execute process. Note: The up arrow key can be used in the command window to repeat previously entered commands and thereby save a lot of key entry. Although we're currently using the error status variable to display an "answer" to some computation, it will normally be set to zero (indicating no errors, consistent with conventions).

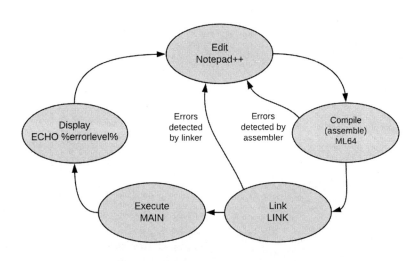

Figure 2.8: Errors found during assembly and linking

Try to introduce a few errors such as use MOVE as the opcode instead of MOV. Also, see what happens when the name of the called function is misspelled. Is the error caught by the assembler or the linker?

Source Code Download

This book contains over 30 program listings as examples of X86-64 coding. I have made them available on the Internet so they can be easily downloaded using the GitHub website. GitHub "is a code hosting platform for version control and collaboration." It is composed of multiple public and private "repositories" holding text, image, and video files. Enter the following command in your Internet browser to initiate the load of all the program listings in this book.

> https://github.com/robertdunne/X64_Asm

I recommend you download and unpack the source code files into the C:\ASM\X64_Asm-master directory which I will be using in examples in the remainder of this book. If you are already familiar with and have experience with GitHub, then use a procedure with which you are most comfortable. Otherwise, please perform the following steps at the GitHub site:

1. Click on the button labeled "Clone or download" which will bring up a drop-down menu.
2. Select "Download Zip" from the drop-down menu which will download one file to your normal downloads directory.
3. You may now exit GitHub or close your browser since you will no longer need it.

From your downloads directory, perform the following to extract all the source code into C:\ASM\X64_Asm-master:

1. Right click on the X64_Asm-master.zip file just downloaded.
2. Select "Extract All..." from the pull-down menu.
3. In the "Select Destination and Extract" screen, change the file name to "C:\Asm64" or the different directory you chose for your work files.
4. Click on the "Extract" button.

The above procedure will generate all of the listing files as TXT files having file names corresponding to the captions under each listing in this book. Each will have to be copied to "main.asm" as needed. In addition, all GitHub repositories should have a README.md file containing pertinent information regarding the rest of the files. For example, the following command prompt generates the main.asm file used in the first demonstration in this chapter:

> copy   X64_Asm-master\Listing_2_1.txt   main.asm

Warning: The assembler source code that appears in this book and is available for download is for learning to program in assembly language. Some of these programs are incomplete and even contain problems that are used as examples. No guarantee of their commercial utility is expressed or implied.

Review Questions

1. What is the difference between source code and object code?
2. Why is there a linker? That is, why don't we go straight from source code to the executable file and skip this "middle man"?
3. Why do you think assembler directives are many times referred to as pseudo instructions?
4. An assembler is an example of a type of compiler. What makes an assembler unique from other compilers?
5. * When updating a line of source code, should the comment on the line be updated as well?

Programming Exercises

1. Modify Listing 2.1 by removing the first line (includelib). Then compile, link, and execute as before. Where was the error caught? Where was it missed?
2. Modify Listing 2.4 so that RCX has a negative number when ExitProcess is called. What happens when you compile, link, and execute?
3. Modify Listing 2.4 by removing the call to ExitProcess on line 9. What happens? Where is the error caught?

— 3 —
Hello World

The "Hello World" program is the "classic" first program students write while learning a new programming language. It simply displays "Hello World" and exits. Chapter 3 will build upon the compile-link-execute sequence for program development introduced in Chapter 2 to actually do something: Read and write text to the command window using Windows API function calls. The X64 Calling Convention and general purpose register use will also be described.

Introductions

Each chapter of this book introduces some X86-64 instructions and/or assembler directives that have not been demonstrated in previous chapters.

X86-64 instructions:

- LEA: Load Effective Address: The 64-bit address of a byte in memory is loaded into a general purpose register.

ML64 directives:

- EQU: The EQU assigns a name to a constant. It not only provides "self documentation," but simplifies changing the constant's value in the future. Using the EQU is like calling your friends by name rather than by their ID numbers.
- LENGTHOF: This function calculates the length of a string at "assembly time."
- .DATA: The .DATA directive marks the beginning of a section in memory which typically contains variable data used while a program runs. It is similar to the .CODE directive (introduced in Chapter 2) which marks the beginning of a section containing X86-64 instructions. Note: Both the .CODE and .DATA directives begin with a period.
- BYTE: The BYTE directive initializes one or more 8-bit bytes in memory. It can build a string of characters as well as a list of numbers smaller than 256.
- QWORD: Initializes one or more "quad words" of memory, each composed of 8 bytes (64 bits).
- DUP: This "assembly time" function duplicates BYTEs, QWORDs, and other basic memory storage units.

Windows API Functions

We've already been using one Windows function, ExitProcess, to quit a program. It is unique in that it does not return control to the instruction after the function call. The new functions that we will be using perform their tasks and then return control to the instruction following the function call.

One of the main responsibilities of an operating system, such as Windows, is to provide an Application Programming Interface (API) for programs. A large number of these functions involves reading and writing peripheral devices (display monitor, keyboard, mouse, network, etc.) and disk files (real spinning disks as well as solid-state memory devices). The calling program must provide Windows with the details of the desired data transfer:

1. What is to be done
2. Which device is to written or read
3. Where is the data located
4. How much data is to be written or read

What is to be done is indicated by the name of the function that is called. In this first example, the WriteConsoleA function is called to write a string of ASCII characters to a command window. Like most current operating systems, the 64-bit Windows functions receive most of the remaining details of the desired data transfer in the CPU's registers.

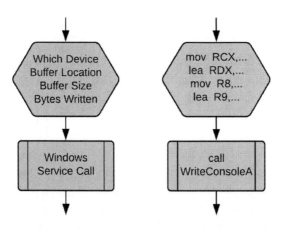

Figure 3.1: Register setup before Windows function call

The WriteConsoleA function displays ASCII characters. The ASCII character code assigns a unique number to each letter, digit, and punctuation mark used in English. Please see Appendix F for more details on ASCII, and see the WriteConsoleW function for displaying Unicode (an extension to ASCII supporting hundreds of languages).

General Purpose Registers

As pointed out in Chapter 1, CPUs contain between about five and one hundred high-performance memory units called registers. The X86-64 CPU has sixteen user-accessible general purpose registers that can be used in computation as well as indexing memory locations. The first eight of these registers are 64-bit extensions of eight registers from the orignal 16-bit Intel 8086. These are referenced in assembly language by their historic names of RAX, RBX, RCX, RDX, RSI, RDI, RBP, and RSP. The remaining eight 64-bit general purpose registers are referenced simply by R8 through R15.

In addition to being general purpose for computation and indexing, Table 3.1 shows many of these registers have a special purpose (either within special CPU instructions or the Windows X64 Calling Convention).

Register	Hardware	Software: X64 Calling Convention
RAX	Default accumulator	Function return value, Volatile
RBX	Index	Nonvolatile
RCX	Loop counter	First integer argument, Volatile
RDX		Second integer argument, Volatile
RSI	Source index	Nonvolatile
RDI	Destination index	Nonvolatile
RBP	"Base" pointer	Nonvolatile
RSP	Stack pointer	Nonvolatile
R8		Third integer argument, Volatile
R9		Fourth integer argument, Volatile
R10		Volatile
R11		Volatile
R12		Nonvolatile
R13		Nonvolatile
R14		Nonvolatile
R15		Nonvolatile

Table 3.1: X86-64 general purpose integer registers (some also have special purpose)

Notes regarding special use of registers:

- Most of the special hardware features described above are carried forward from 16-bit versions of the Intel 8086.

- The above registers can be divided in half and quarter. Registers EAX, AX, AL, and AH are all fractions of the 64-bit RAX register. These fractions will be demonstrated in Chapter 7.
- The assignment of registers for calling 64-bit Microsoft Windows functions and C++ functions is rather different than what was used in previous versions of Windows. The old 32-bit applications run in the 64-bit versions of Windows (Windows 7 and 10) in an emulation mode known as WOW (Windows On Windows). The 16-bit applications will not even run on a modern Windows-based computer.

The X86-64 architecture contains additional registers used for parallel processing of data and floating point operations. These are not needed in elementary assembly language programs and will not be introduced until later chapters.

X64 Calling Convention

Procedures, including Windows API functions and C++ functions, are entered simply by executing the "machine code" CALL instruction. However, procedures need to be told what to do, and that is done using software calling conventions. The parameters needed, such as which device to read and write as well as how much data is to be transferred, is passed to the procedure in "arguments." In 32-bit Windows, there were several "standards" for passing arguments, which really meant there was not a commonplace standard at all.

For 64-bit Windows, Microsoft uses the Application Binary Interface (ABI) popular in other operating systems which is basically the same as its own "fast call" standard in 32-bit Windows. There are basically three requirements for meeting the X64 Calling Convention:

1. Location of arguments: The first four arguments are passed in registers RCX, RDX, R8, R9, respectively. If more than four arguments, then they will be pushed onto the stack. See Chapter 13 for floating point arguments and arguments on the stack.
2. Volatile registers: The calling program assumes registers RAX, RCX, RDX, and R8 through R11 are volatile (i.e., they will be modified and not saved by the procedure). The contents of registers RBX, RSI, RDI, RBP, RSP, and R12 through R15 are considered non-volatile (i.e., they will have the same contents on return from the procedure as when the procedure was called). Functions return values in RAX.
3. Shadow space: The called procedure assumes the stack contains room for storing four 64-bit registers (32 bytes total). Also, it is assumed that the RSP stack pointer will be aligned on a 128-bit (16 byte) address boundary. Because the CALL instruction pushes its return address (8 bytes) onto the stack, a shadow space of 40 bytes is typically reserved on the stack before each procedure call in order to meet both the storage and alignment requirements.

Stack Pointer (RSP) Register

The RSP register points to the "top" of the stack, an area of memory where temporary data may be stored. In the mid-1970s, computers, such as the DEC PDP 11, implemented the concept of a stack using PUSH, POP, and CALL machine code instructions. Characteristics of a stack:

- A common metaphor of stack operation is the placing and getting of cafeteria trays and plates. You place new trays on top and also remove trays from the top. Who would try to take the tray on the very bottom or from the middle of a stack?
- Data is stored onto and retrieved from the stack in a LIFO (Last In, First Out) manner. Stack usage is very easy: You "push" new data onto the stack and "pop" the most recent data from the top of the stack. The pushing and popping user does not have to know the details of where in memory the stack is actually located and exactly how it works.
- Pushing the contents of an X86-64 register onto the stack results in the RSP register being decreased by 8. Most operating systems, including Windows, fill their stacks from high memory addresses to lower addresses.
- The RSP pointer is initialized by Windows when it starts each program. It is possible for a user program to push more data onto the stack than Windows allocated, but this rarely happens and usually caused by a serious programming error.

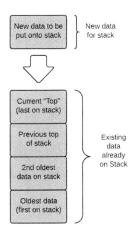

Figure 3.2: Stack "concept"

What do we mean by "pushing data on top of the stack" or "popping data from the top of the stack"?

Figure 3.2 illustrates pushing a value onto a stack that already contains four values. The size of each value can vary among applications and CPU architectures. In the X86-64, the PUSH instruction not only stores 64-bits onto the stack area of memory, but also updates the RSP register. The POP instruction does the reverse: It loads a 64-bit register from data in memory and also updates the RSP.

Parameters and Arguments

Windows functions have a list of parameters (i.e., variables) that dictate what is to be done. This parameter data is passed to the Windows function in what is commonly referred to as arguments. For example, "parameter 1" is passed to the function in "argument 1," which in the X64 Calling Convention is located in register RCX. Arguments are generally of two types:

1. Pass by value: The argument is contained in the register or stack.
2. Pass by reference: The argument is in memory and is pointed to by an address in a register or on the stack.

Hello World Example

The main.asm program will now be upgraded to display "Hello World" in the command window. The source code file, as shown in Listing 3.1, can be downloaded from GitHub or simply be updated from the last main.asm source file in Chapter 2. The following lines support new features:

- Lines 2 and 3: Two new Windows functions will be called: GetStdHandle opens a device or file, while WriteConsoleA will write ASCII text data to it.
- Line 4: A "handle" will be attached to each device or file that is read or written by the program. The device code value of -11 selects the CMD window output display.
- Line 10: Meets the specification of the X64 Calling Convention for shadow memory. Note that space is reserved by decreasing the stack pointer. Before this main program exits, it will have to remove the reserved space (see line 26).
- Lines 12 through 16: The GetStdHandle function is called with one argument (device code in RCX) and returns a file handle in register RAX, which is then saved in memory. The file handle will be needed when calling WriteConsoleA to write to the CMD window.
- Lines 18 through 24: Only four arguments are needed, so they are all loaded into the registers: two passed by value using the MOV instruction and two passed by reference using the LEA instruction. After performing this service, the Windows API function returns the number of bytes transferred to the calling program in a quad word (64-bits) in memory pointed to by register R9.
- Line 26: The shadow space on the stack is removed.
- Line 32: The .data directive tells the assembler that the following lines of text should be grouped in a portion of memory along with other variable data.
- Line 33: The label "msg" is the name by which the address of a string of ASCII letters in memory containing "Hello World" can be

referenced.

- Lines 34 and 35: From an X86-64 perspective, a byte is 8-bits, a word is 16-bits, a double word is 32-bits, and a quad word is 64-bits. Labels stdout and nbwr refer to the addresses of data storage for 64-bit values. The question marks indicate that no initial values are expected to be loaded into memory for these data.

```
1.                    includelib  kernel32.lib        ; Windows kernel interface.
2. GetStdHandle       proto                           ; Function to retrieve I/O handle
3. WriteConsoleA      proto                           ; Function writes to command window
4. Console            equ         -11                 ; Device code for console text output.
5. ExitProcess        proto
6.
7.                    .code
8. main               proc
9.
10.                   sub         RSP,40              ; Reserve "shadow space" on stack.
11.
12. ;                 Obtain "handle" for console display monitor I/O streams
13.
14.                   mov         RCX,Console         ; Console standard output handle
15.                   call        GetStdHandle        ; Returns handle in register RAX
16.                   mov         stdout,RAX          ; Save handle for text display.
17.
18. ;                 Display the "Hello World" message.
19.
20.                   mov         RCX,stdout          ; Handle to standard output device
21.                   lea         RDX,msg             ; Pointer to message (byte array).
22.                   mov         R8,lengthof msg     ; Number of characters to display
23.                   lea         R9,nbwr             ; Number of bytes actually written.
24.                   call        WriteConsoleA       ; Write text to command window.
25.
26.                   add         RSP,40              ; Replace "shadow space" on stack
27.                   mov         RCX,0               ; Set exit status code to zero.
28.                   call        ExitProcess         ; Return control to Windows.
29.
30. main              endp
31.
32.                   .data
33. msg               byte        "Hello World"
34. stdout            qword       ?                   ; Handle to standard output device
35. nbwr              qword       ?                   ; Number of bytes actually written
36.
37.                   end
```

Listing 3.1: Program to display "Hello World" in the command console.

Listing 3.2 shows the compile-link-execute of the Hello World program. The first line sets the path to the directory containing the assembler and linker (see Chapter 2). The second line assumes the source code was downloaded from GitHub as demonstrated in Chapter 2. I will no longer be using the echo command to display answers since we will now be outputting with WriteConsoleA.

```
C:\ASM64> PATH  C:\######\Hostx64\x64;%PATH%
C:\ASM64> COPY  X64_Asm-master\Listing_3_1.txt  main.asm
1 file(s) copied.
C:\ASM64> ML64 main.asm /link /SUBSYSTEM:CONSOLE /ENTRY:main
Microsoft (R) Macro Assembler (x64) Version 14.11.25547.0
Copyright (C) Microsoft Corporation. All rights reserved.

Assembling: main.asm
Microsoft (R) Incremental Linker Version 14.11.25547.0
Copyright (C) Microsoft Corporation. All rights reserved.

/OUT:main.exe
main.obj
/SUBSYSTEM:CONSOLE
/ENTRY:main

C:\ASM64>main
Hello World
C:\ASM64>
```

Listing 3.2: Command lines to build and execute "Hello World" program

Read and Write

The main.asm program will now be upgraded to both read and write text data. ReadConsoleA is a Windows API function that reads from the keyboard (or redirected disk files or I/O device). The following register contents will be set before the ReadConsoleA function is called:

1. RCX: Value of the device code for keyboard input
2. RDX: Reference points to memory buffer to be filled from keyboard
3. R8: Value of the maximum number of bytes to be read.
4. R9: Reference points to a 64-bit memory location to receive number of bytes actually read.

In the next program listing, new features are on the following lines:

- Line 4: A new Windows function will be called: ReadConsoleA will

read ASCII text data from keyboard using the command window..
- Line 6: A "handle" will be attached to each device or file that is read or written by program. The device code value of -10 selects the CMD window keyboard input.
- Lines 18 through 25: The GetStdHandle function is called twice: Once to get a handle for console display output and next to get a handle for keyboard input. There is one argument (device code in RCX), and the function returns a file handle in register RAX, which is then saved in memory. The file handles will be needed when calling ReadConsoleA and WriteConsoleA.
- Lines 27 through 33: This is the same as the previous "Hello World" output except the message is now "Please enter text message."

```
 1.              includelib  kernel32.lib   ; Windows kernel interface.
 2. GetStdHandle  proto                     ; Function to retrieve I/O handles
 3. WriteConsoleA proto                     ; Function writes to command window
 4. ReadConsoleA  proto                     ; Function reads keyboard buffer
 5. Console       equ       -11             ; Device code for console text output
 6. Keyboard      equ       -10             ; Device code for console text input
 7. ExitProcess   proto
 8.
 9.              .code
10.
11. ;           Main program that reads text message from user through command
12. ;           window keyin and displays it in same command window.
13.
14. main         proc
15.
16.              sub       RSP,40           ; Reserve "shadow space" on stack.
17.
18. ;           Obtain "handles" for console I/O streams
19.
20.              mov       RCX,Console      ; Console standard output handle
21.              call      GetStdHandle     ; Returns handle in register RAX
22.              mov       stdout,RAX       ; Save handle of console display.
23.              mov       RCX,Keyboard     ; Console standard input handle
24.              call      GetStdHandle     ; Returns handle in register RAX
25.              mov       stdin,RAX        ; Save handle for keyboard input.
26.
27. ;           Display the prompt message.
28.
29.              mov       RCX,stdout       ; Handle to standard output device
30.              lea       RDX,pmsg         ; Pointer to prompt message
31.              mov       R8,lengthof msg  ; Number of characters to display
32.              lea       R9,nbwr          ; Number of bytes actually written.
33.              call      WriteConsoleA    ; Write text string to command box.
34.
```

35. ;		Read input line from user keyboard.	
36.			
37.	mov	RCX,stdin	; Handle to standard input device
38.	mov	R8,20	; Maximum length to receive
39.	lea	RDX,keymsg	; Memory address to receive input
40.	lea	R9,nbrd	; Number of bytes actually read.
41.	call	ReadConsoleA	; Read text string from command box.
42.			
43. ;		Echo the message input back to the user.	
44.			
45.	mov	RCX,stdout	; Handle to standard output device
46.	lea	RDX,keymsg	; Pointer to message that was input
47.	mov	R8,nbrd	; Length (bytes) of input message
48.	lea	R9,nbwr	; Number of bytes actually written.
49.	call	WriteConsoleA	; Write text string to command box.
50.			
51.	add	RSP,40	; Replace "shadow space" on stack
52.	mov	RCX,0	; Set exit status code to zero.
53.	call	ExitProcess	; Return control to Windows.
54.			
55. main	endp		
56.			
57.	.data		
58. pmsg	byte	"Please enter text message: "	
59. keymsg	byte	20 DUP (?)	; Memory buffer for keyboard input
60. stdout	qword	?	; Handle to standard output device
61. nbwr	qword	?	; Number of bytes actually written
62. stdin	qword	?	; Handle to standard input device
63. nbrd	qword	?	; Number of bytes actually read
64.			
65.	end		

Listing 3.3: Program that echos keyboard input to a command console window

- Lines 35 through 41: The ReadConsoleA function is called to place keyboard input into memory buffer keymsg. The quad word in memory, pointed to by register R9, will be returned with the number of characters entered (including carriage return and line feed).
- Lines 43 through 49: The message just input will now be displayed in a manner similar to the prompt.

Listing 3.4 shows the compile-link-execute of the Read and Write program. As in the previous example, the first line sets the path to the directory containing the assembler and linker, while the second line assumes the source code was downloaded from GitHub. It is then assembled and linked as before. When this new program runs, it waits for user input, which it then echoes back to the console display and exits.

```
C:\ASM64> path  C:\######\Hostx64\x64;%PATH%
C:\ASM64> copy  X64_Asm-master\Listing_3_3.txt  main.asm
1 file(s) copied.
C:\ASM64> ml64 main.asm /link /SUBSYSTEM:CONSOLE /ENTRY:main
Microsoft (R) Macro Assembler (x64) Version 14.11.25547.0
Copyright (C) Microsoft Corporation. All rights reserved.

Assembling: main.asm
Microsoft (R) Incremental Linker Version 14.11.25547.0
Copyright (C) Microsoft Corporation. All rights reserved.

/OUT:main.exe
main.obj
/SUBSYSTEM:CONSOLE
/ENTRY:main

C:\ASM64>main
Please enter text message: Short echo test
Short echo test
C:\ASM64>
```

Listing 3.4: Console program to read and write one text line

The last few lines in Listing 3.4 show the program execution where the text string "Short echo test" is keyed in followed by the "enter key." Try other messages, especially one that is longer than 20 characters. See the Review Questions and Programming Exercises section for some more ideas to test this program.

Unicode

ASCII is a 7-bit code containing a total of 128 letters, digits, punctuation marks, and control characters. Unicode is a super set of ASCII (the first 128 characters are the same) supporting many languages from around the world. The first 65,536 characters of Unicode are stored in memory as 16-bit words and displayed with the WriteConsoleW function call. The following changes are necessary to run the above "Hello World" program with Unicode (see Programming Exercise 1 for details and example).

1. Change WriteConsoleA to WriteConsoleW
2. Change the byte directive to word directive (8-bits to 16-bits)
3. Message must be entered as individual letters rather than a single string. Non-ASCII characters can be looked up in Unicode tables on the Internet and entered as hexadecimal.

Review Questions

1. What are two important resources provided by an operating system such as Windows?
2. What type of argument (pass by value or pass by reference) enables Windows functions to return values to a calling program?
3. * In the C language, a "function" is an extension of a "procedure" that allows the return of a single value associated with the function, such as Y = SQRT(X). Where do you think the return value is located within the X64 Calling Convention?
4. Why must a string of ten ASCII characters be passed by reference and not by value?
5. What happens when more than the maximum number of characters is entered (value of 20 on line 38 of Listing 3.3)? Try it.
6. What happens when the size of the buffer is smaller than the maximum size passed to ReadConsoleA (Listing 3.3 having a value on line 38 being greater than the value on line 59)? What then happens when the number of characters entered is greater than the buffer size? How could the "lengthof" directive be used to eliminate this problem?
7. * The 40 bytes of shadow space meet the requirements for alignment and room to store four 64-bit registers. What else is assumed to make this value of 40 work (the alignment requirement in particular)?

Programming Exercises

1. Modify Listing 3.1 to output in Unicode: Change lines 3 and 24 to WriteConsoleW. Change the directive on line 33 from byte to word, and change "Hello World" to "H", "e", "l", "l", "o", " ", "W", "o", "r", "l", "d" where each letter will now use 16-bits. Then compile, link, and execute as before. This example shows that the first 128 characters of Unicode are the same as 7-bit ASCII. Now substitute in some other Unicode characters such as a Greek lambda (hexadecimal code 3bb entered as 03bbh) instead of the "l" in Hello. Try some other Unicode character codes for some variety.
2. Change the repeat count on line 59 of Listing 3.3 from 20 to 2. Recompile, link, execute, and enter "World" in response to the prompt. What happened? Register RAX has a completion status of the last call to WriteConsoleA. Use a "MOV RCX,RAX" before the call to ExitProcess so that this value can be examined using the echo command. Change the repeat count back to 20, and check the status again.

— 4 —
Loops & Branches

Having versatility while performing repetitive tasks characterizes much of computer software applications. Chapter 4 introduces instructions and special registers that make the use of "loops" and conditional "branches" perform repetitive tasks effectively.

Introductions

The Compare (CMP) and Jump if Greater (GT) instructions are introduced to control program flow. They use the RFLAGS and RIP registers to control the flow of computer programs. Several other conditional jumps and moves will also be described with some examples in the Programming Exercises.

- CMP: Compare: The contents of a 64-bit register are compared to an immediate integer value, contents of another register, or contents of a memory location. This is basically a subtraction instruction where the answer is not stored anywhere.
- JG: Jump if Greater: Program flow normally proceeds from one instruction to the next one immediately after it in memory. However, "jump" instructions provide a means to go to another part of the program. Instructions such as JG only jump to a new program location if various conditions are met. JG requires a previous arithmetic instruction, such as subtract or compare, to have a non-negative result.
- INC: Increment by 1: The value in a register is incremented by 1. This is basically an addition instruction, but it executes slightly faster, and it will also set the status flags.
- DEC: Decrement by 1: The value in a register is decremented by 1. This is basically a subtraction instruction, but it executes slightly faster, and it will also set the status flags.

Program Loops

Computers are great for doing repetitive operations. A loop is a "process" that can be performed multiple times until a "decision" is made to move onto something else. Examples of processes and decisions:

- Process: Eating one mouthful of food at lunch
- Decision: Is there any more food on my plate?

- Process: Grading one student's exam
- Decision: Are there any more exams to grade?

- Process: Display one bit ("0" or "1") on the monitor
- Decision: Are there any more bits remaining to display?

A loop consists of three parts:

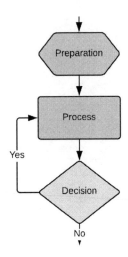

Figure 4.1: Program loop

1. Preparation: Set initial values for a) variables to be modified during each pass of the loop and b) variables, like counters, that will determine when to exit the loop.
2. A process to be repeated multiple times: Examples include adding numbers to a running total, searching a table for a particular value, and calling the same set of subroutines multiple times.
3. Decision when to exit the loop: Some loops such as those used in a medical device performing real-time life-support are not intended to stop. However, most loops do have an exit objective such as all of the desired set of numbers have been added, the entire table has been searched, the desired value has been located, etc.

The main program from Chapter 3 will now be modified to repeatedly echo lines of input text until an empty line is entered. If only the "enter" key is entered, the number of bytes transfered will be two: carriage return and line feed. Listing 4.1 contains the following modifications to Listing 3.3 from Chapter 3:

- Line 7: MaxBuf is an assembly-time equate to set the maximum keyboard buffer size. It will be used in both the call to ReadConsoleA (line 41) and the memory space allocation (line 68).
- Lines 14,15: Comments are expanded to explain what the program is doing.
- Line 32: Label "nxtlin" is added to mark the top of the loop where the prompt message is displayed. Notice: There is a colon after labels on the instructions.

```
1.                      includelib  kernel32.lib      ; Windows kernel interface.
2. GetStdHandle        proto                          ; Function to retrieve I/O handles
3. WriteConsoleA       proto                          ; Function writes to CMD window
4. ReadConsoleA        proto                          ; Function reads CMD window
5. Console             equ        -11                 ; Device code for console text output
6. Keyboard            equ        -10                 ; Device code for console text input
7. MaxBuf              equ        20                  ; Maximum input buffer size
8. ExitProcess         proto
9.
10.                     .code
11.
12. ;                   Main program that reads text message from user through command
13. ;                   window keyin and displays it in same command window.
14. ;                             1. Multiple lines input until only "Enter" key pushed.
15. ;                             2. Each line will be echoed on a separate line in display.
16.
17. main                proc
18.
19.                     sub        RSP,40             ; Reserve "shadow space" on stack.
20.
21. ;                   Obtain "handles" for console I/O streams
22.
23.                     mov        RCX,Console        ; Console standard output handle
24.                     call       GetStdHandle       ; Returns handle in register RAX
25.                     mov        stdout,RAX         ; Save handle of console display.
26.                     mov        RCX,Keyboard       ; Console standard input handle
27.                     call       GetStdHandle       ; Returns handle in register RAX
28.                     mov        stdin,RAX          ; Save handle for keyboard input.
29.
30. ;                   Display the prompt message.
31.
32. nxtlin:             mov        RCX,stdout         ; Handle to standard output device
33.                     lea        RDX,msg            ; Pointer to prompt message
34.                     mov        R8,lengthof msg    ; Number of characters to display
35.                     lea        R9,nbwr            ; Number of bytes actually written.
36.                     call       WriteConsoleA      ; Write text string to command box.
37.
38. ;                   Read input line from user keyboard.
39.
40.                     mov        RCX,stdin          ; Handle to standard input device
41.                     mov        R8,MaxBuf          ; Maximum length to receive
42.                     lea        RDX,keymsg         ; Memory address to receive input
43.                     lea        R9,nbrd            ; Number of bytes actually read.
44.                     call       ReadConsoleA       ; Read text string from command box.
45.
46. ;                   Echo the message input back to the user.
47.
48.                     mov        RCX,stdout         ; Handle to standard output device
49.                     lea        RDX,keymsg         ; Pointer to message that was input
```

50.	mov	R8,nbrd	; Length (bytes) of input message
51.	lea	R9,nbwr	; Number of bytes actually written.
52.	call	WriteConsoleA	; Write text string to command box.
53.			
54. ;		Go get another line, but exit if only "Enter" key was input.	
55.			
56.	mov	R8,nbrd	; Length (bytes) of input message
57.	cmp	R8,2	; Test if only CR and LF characters.
58.	jg	nxtlin	; Loop back around for next input.
59.			
60.	add	RSP,40	; Replace "shadow space" on stack
61.	mov	RCX,0	; Set exit status code to zero.
62.	call	ExitProcess	; Return control to Windows.
63.			
64. main	endp		
65.			
66.	.data		
67. msg	byte	"Please enter text message: "	
68. keymsg	byte	MaxBuf DUP (?)	; Memory buffer for keyboard input
69. stdout	qword	?	; Handle to standard output device
70. nbwr	qword	?	; Number of bytes actually written
71. stdin	qword	?	; Handle to standard input device
72. nbrd	qword	?	; Number of bytes actually read
73.			
74.	end		

Listing 4.1: Program echoes lines of input text until empty line received.

- Lines 54 through 58: Bottom of the loop: Here the number of bytes received from ReadConsoleA is compared to the immediate value of 2. If the count is greater than 2, then jump back to the instruction at label nxtlin.

```
C:\ASM64>main
Please enter text message: Short echo test
Short echo test
Please enter text message: Another line 12345
Another line 12345
Please enter text message:

C:\ASM64>
```

Listing 4.2: Loop of multiple input text lines echoed

The program in Listing 4.1 may also be obtained through the GitHub copy as was done in Listing 3.4. The compile and link steps are exactly the same as in previous chapters, so they will no longer be shown unless changes are needed.

Listing 4.2 shows the running of the new program with two lines of text being entered from the keyboard and echoed. The third input line is only the "enter" key, thereby forcing the program to exit.

Nested Loops

Let's modify the program again to make it a bit more interesting. This time, we will display each character on a separate line.

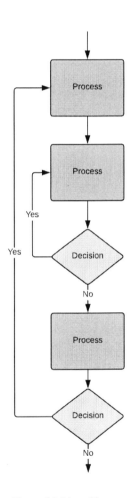

A very common programming technique is one loop nested within another. Each loop will have its own exit condition.

- The outer loop will be similar to the previous example: The user will be prompted for an input which will then be echoed back to the user on the display monitor.
- The inner loop adds the new feature in this example where each character will be on its own line. The inner loop will have register R12 initialized to point to the first character in the buffer, and also have register R13 initialized to the number of characters input.

Although nested loops are a powerful technique, it's very easy to write large nested loops with confusing code where one loop's data and counters interfere with that of the other.

Figure 4.2: Nested loops

The first 45 lines of the program will remain the same, so to save space and focus on the loops, Listing 4.3 will begin on line 29 at the top of the outer loop. The only alteration needed to the program is to convert the echo of the input line to be split among several individual output lines. Here's a hint where I'm heading with this: Each of these lines will eventually contain not only the single ASCII character, but its binary, hexadecimal, and decimal representation as well.

The following lines are of interest in Listing 4.3:

- Lines 30 through 70: Outer loop that prompts for keyboard input and echoes it one character per line until an empty line is entered.
- Lines 46 through 64: Inner loop that echoes the input text line, one character at a time, followed by a carriage return and line feed.
- Lines 51 through 55: Display one character of text line that was input.
- Lines 57 through 61: Display end of line characters.
- Line 62: Increment memory buffer pointer to next character (same as ADD R12,1).
- Line 63: Decrement number of characters to be displayed. This instruction also sets the flags needed for the JG instructions that follows on line 64.
- Line 81: A string of carriage return (hex 0D) and line feed (hex 0A) ASCII control characters.

```
29.
30. ;          Display the prompt message.
31.
32. nxtlin:   mov     RCX,stdout        ; Handle to standard output device
33.           lea     RDX,msg           ; Pointer to prompt message
34.           mov     R8,lengthof msg   ; Number of characters to display
35.           lea     R9,nbwr           ; Number of bytes actually written.
36.           call    WriteConsoleA     ; Write text string to command box.
37.
38. ;          Read input line from user keyboard.
39.
40.           mov     RCX,stdin         ; Handle to standard input device
41.           mov     R8,MaxBuf         ; Maximum length to receive
42.           lea     RDX,keymsg        ; Memory address to receive input
43.           lea     R9,nbrd           ; Number of bytes actually read.
44.           call    ReadConsoleA      ; Read text entered from keyboard.
45.
46. ;          Echo line just input back to the user one character at a time.
47.
48.           lea     R12,keymsg        ; Memory buffer containing input
49.           mov     R13,nbrd          ; Number of characters actually read
50.
51. inloop:   mov     RCX,stdout        ; Handle to standard output device
52.           mov     RDX,R12           ; Point to next character to display
```

53.	mov	R8,1	; Only display 1 character.
54.	lea	R9,nbwr	; Number of bytes actually written.
55.	call	WriteConsoleA	; Write text string to command box.
56.			
57.	mov	RCX,stdout	; Handle to standard output device
58.	lea	RDX,newln	; Point buffer containing CR and LF.
59.	mov	R8,2	; Length of CR/LF buffer.
60.	lea	R9,nbwr	; Number of bytes actually written.
61.	call	WriteConsoleA	; Write text string to command box.
62.	inc	R12	; Set pointer to next character.
63.	dec	R13	; Decrement remaining byte count.
64.	jg	inloop	; Loop until message complete.
65.			
66. ;		Go get another line, but exit if only "Enter" key was input.	
67.			
68.	mov	R8,nbrd	; Length (bytes) of input message
69.	cmp	R8,2	; Test if only CR and LF characters.
70.	jg	nxtlin	; Loop back for another input.
71.			
72.	add	RSP,40	; Replace "shadow space" on stack
73.	mov	RCX,0	; Set exit status code to zero.
74.	call	ExitProcess	; Return control to Windows.
75.			
76. main	endp		
77.			
78.	.data		
79. msg	byte	"Please enter text message: "	
80. keymsg	byte	MaxBuf DUP (?)	; Memory buffer for keyboard input
81. newln	byte	0DH,0AH	; Carriage return and line feed
82. stdout	qword	?	; Handle to standard output device
83. nbwr	qword	?	; Number of bytes actually written
84. stdin	qword	?	; Handle to standard input device
85. nbrd	qword	?	; Number of bytes actually read
86.			
87.	end		

Listing 4.3: Program to echo each character on its own line.

Why did I use registers R12 and R13 to hold the buffer pointer and remaining byte count? Why not use R10 and R11, for example? As described in Chapter 3, the Windows API functions abide by the X64 Calling Convention. The contents of registers R12 and R13 are guaranteed to be preserved (i.e, non-volatile) by the call to WriteConsoleA, while the contents of volatile registers, such as R10 and R11, are not.

Go ahead and compile, link, and execute the program in Listing 4.3 as you did in the previous examples. Your output will be similar to that appearing next in Listing 4.4.

```
C:\ASM64>main
Please enter text message: First line
F
i
r
s
t

l
i
n
e

Please enter text message: Last
L
a
s
t

Please enter text message:

C:\ASM64>
```

Listing 4.4: Echo each character on its own line.

RIP and RFLAGS Registers

We have been working with the general purpose registers, all of which can be modified using the move and arithmetic instructions, but there are two special purpose registers that we have been using indirectly. The RIP Instruction Pointer provides the memory location of the next instruction to be executed. In the X86-64 architecture, the RIP is automatically incremented as each instruction is executed. Jump and call instructions explicitly change the value of the RIP register.

Historically, about half the CPU architectures refer to their instruction pointers as IP registers, while half refer to them as PC (Program Counter) registers. Some architectures even allow "move" instructions to alter the PC or IP, but even if they do, I highly recommend not doing so.

Nearly every CPU ever designed has a Processor State Register which provides information regarding previous instructions that were executed (as well as other status info):

1. Was the previous result zero?
2. Was the previous result positive or negative?

3. Did the previous result fit within the register size?
4. Did the instruction end in error (like the sum of two positive numbers resulting in a negative number)?

In the X86-64 architecture, there are many status flag bits, and they primarily reside in the RFLAGS register. Table 4.1 contains the status flag bits that are used by jump instructions and are set by arithmetic, logic, and compare instructions. The actual locations of these bits are not important at this point because the jump instructions know where they are, and software generally should not be setting them directly.

Z	Zero: Result was zero (i.e., bits 63..0 = 0)
S	Sign: Result was negative (same as high order bit, i.e., bit 63 = 1)
C	Carry: Result is a value that exceeded 64 bit register.
O	Overflow: Result overflowed into sign bit.
P	Parity: Lower 8 bits of result has even parity (count of 1-bits).

Table 4.1: Status flag bits used by jump instructions

Both "carry" and "overflow" indicate possible problems in the high order bits (left side) of a binary number. For example, if we had a 4-bit register, and I added binary 1000 to 1000, I would get 10000 which obviously does not fit because it requires five bits. This situation is referred to as carry.

If in the same 4-bit register, I added 0100 to 0100, I would get 1000, which fits, but might indicate a problem. If I consider my numbers to be unsigned, I have decimal 4 plus 4 equals 8, but if I consider my numbers to be signed, I then have 4 plus 4 equals negative 8, which is definitely wrong. The CPU will set the overflow flag, and it does not care or even know whether I am using unsigned or signed numbers. It is up to the software to decide if the overflow is an error or not. Please see Appendix G for more details if you like.

Jump Instructions

In Listing 4.1 and 4.3, I only used the JG (Jump if Greater) jump instruction. However, the X86 architecture supports a wide variety of jump instructions based on the current values of various flags. There is also an unconditional jump (JMP) which says change the RIP to the new value irregardless of any of the flags.

- JMP: Jump (no conditions needed)

The jumps in the following list depend on whether a single flag is set (value=1) or not set (i.e., clear, value=0).

- JZ, JE: Jump if Zero, Jump if Equal
- JNZ, JNE: Jump if Not Zero, Jump if Not Equal
- JS: Jump on Sign
- JNS: Jump on Not Sign
- JC: Jump on Carry
- JNC: Jump on Not Carry
- JO: Jump on Overflow
- JNO: Jump on Not Overflow
- JP, JPE: Jump on Parity, Jump if Parity Even
- JNP, JPO: Jump if Not Parity, Jump if Parity Odd

The assembler produces exactly the same machine code whether JZ (Jump if Zero) or JE (Jump if Equal) is used. This flexibility enables the programmer to "self document" what is being done. It doesn't replace a good comment, but it does enhance it. For example, if I wrote a program that compared R12 to the value 137, and R12 did contain 137, then the Z-flag would have been set. However, the Z-flag could also have been set if I subtracted down to zero. In the first case JE or JNE would be more appropriate, and in the latter case, JZ or JNZ would be best.

Except in unusually cases, I only use the JMP, JZ, JE, JNZ, and JNE in the above list. The jump on parity was a more popular instruction decades ago, when the CPU software might be performing data communications error checking. The other jumps using the carry and sign flags are better described in the following list. Note: CF=1 implies the carry flag is set, OF=1 implies the overflow flag is set, and ZF=1 implies the zero flag is set.

- JA, JNBE: Jump if Above, Jump if Not Below or Equal
  (CF = 0 AND ZF = 0)
- JAE, JNB: Jump if Above or Equal, Jump if Not Below
  (CF = 0)
- JB, JNAE: Jump if Below, Jump if Not Above or Equal
  (CF = 1)
- JBE, JNA: Jump if Below or Equal, Jump if Not Above
  (CF = 1 OR ZF = 1)
- JG, JNLE: Jump if Greater, Jump if Not Less or Equal
  (SF = OF AND ZF = 0)
- JGE, JNL: Jump if Greater or Equal, Jump if Not Less
  (SF = OF)
- JL, JNGE: Jump if Less, Jump if Not Greater or Equal
  (SF != OF; i.e., Sign Flag not equal to Overflow Flag)
- JLE, JNG: Jump if Less or Equal, Jump if Not Greater
  (SF != OF OR ZF = 1)

Some new programmers are confused by the difference between JA (Jump Above) and JG (Jump Greater). The flags show the exact difference, but generally JA is used for unsigned numbers, and JG works with signed numbers. Actually, the CPU has no idea if the program is working with signed or unsigned integers. That's one of the main benefits of using one's complement or two's complement hardware to represent numbers instead of the sign and magnitude approach. Please see Appendix G and Chapter 7 for more details on binary representation for a further explanation.

Conditional Move

Conditional move instructions were added to the X86 instruction set as it evolved from the original 8086 to today's X86-64. Basically, there exists a conditional move instruction corresponding to each of the conditions in the jump instructions. For example: JZ => CMOVZ, JNZ => CMOVNZ, down through JLE => CMOVLE. Using these conditional moves whenever possible has a twofold advantage over an equivalent "jump-over" technique: The code is easier to read for us humans, and it executes faster (two reasons for speed improvement, see Review Question 6).

Table 4.2 shows a conditional move instruction on the left and the "jump-over" technique it replaces on the right.

CMP	AX,10		CMP	AX,10
CMOVG	AX,10		JLE	overIt
			MOV	AX,10

Table 4.2: Compare conditional move to "jump over"

LOOP and JCXZ

The X86-64 instruction set actually contains an instruction named LOOP which was designed for implementing loops. Why didn't I use that one instruction instead of the two instructions: CMP and JG? See Review Question 7 for the best answer, but a subtle answer is that the LOOP instruction was designed to improve the performance of 8086 processors, and in many situations in today's CPUs, it will actually run a little slower than the two instructions I used. I do, however, like the self documentation that comes from the name "loop."

There are also a few instructions such as JCXZ which jump based on whether the current contents of the CX "count" register are zero (i.e., doesn't examine the flags). The JECXZ and JRCXZ are the corresponding 32-bit and 64-bit extensions which jump if register ECX is zero or register RCX is zero, respectively.

Review Questions

1. Why are loops important in a computer program?
2. What's an infinite loop? How does one happen? Why would we intentionally create an infinite loop?
3. How can the addition of two positive numbers result in a negative number? Which status bit would be set indicating this error occurred?
4. The X86 architecture has a TEST instruction which is basically a logical AND that does not store its result. Provide an example when a TEST instruction would be used instead of a CMP compare instruction?
5. The CALL and RET instructions are actually unconditional jump instructions. How are they different from JMP? How can a CALL be replaced by a JMP instruction?
6. The conditional move instructions save instruction execution time by using one instruction rather than two, but they can also improve pipe-lining performance. From a quick Internet search, why do you think jump instructions flush the pipeline and conditional move instructions do not?
7. * On lines 63 and 64 of Listing 4.3, a DEC followed by a JG was used to continue the loop. Why wasn't a LOOP instruction used instead?

Programming Exercises

1. The inner loop in Listing 4.3 is terminated when R13 counts down to zero on lines 63 and 64. Instead, terminate the loop when R12 points to the last character input (a line feed character). There may, of course, be a problem if no line feed character is present, so it's a good thing that a carriage return and line feed immediately follow the input buffer in the data area.
2. Modify Listing 4.3 to combine the display of a single input character (line 55) with the display of carriage return and line feed (line 61). Make a new data "byte" variable named "echo," and place it immediately before the "newlin" data on line 81. Instead of lines 51 through 55 calling WriteConsleA, copy the value pointed to by register R12 to the new "echo" variable, and output three bytes from "echo" on line 61.

— 5 —
Macros & Subroutines

One of the principal hallmarks of the industrial revolution was the use of interchangeable parts in the manufacturing process. In a similar manner, subroutines, macros, and operating system Application Programming Interfaces (API) are building blocks for developing large sophisticated software applications. These three building blocks are predefined program segments that can be used over and over again by calling them from the application program.

- API Function: A section of operating system code that is called ("jumped to") to perform a common task for all user programs.
- Subroutine: A section of user-written code that is called to perform a common task within a user program.
- Macro: A section of user-written code that is essentially "copied and pasted" into multiple locations within the program source code.

Introductions

We're only performing structural changes in Chapter 5, so only a few new directives and one new instruction appear in the code.

X86-64 instructions:

- RET: Return: Subroutines are entered by a CALL instruction which pushes a "return address" onto the stack just like the Windows functions have been entered. The RET instruction effectively pops the return address from the stack into the RIP register, thereby returning to the instruction after the call.

ML64 directives:

- MACRO: The MACRO directive marks the beginning, provides a name, and identifies parameters for a macro.
- ENDM: The end of a macro is indicated by ENDM.
- OFFSET: Get address of data variable.

Macros

A macro is similar to "copy and paste." A macro is a series of assembly language instructions and directives that is given a name. Whenever that name appears later in the program source code in the opcode column, the series of instructions and directives is substituted. Macros not only enable quicker initial program development, but also provide better documentation and maintenance. Some flexibility is provided by giving the macro a list of parameters that can be changed whenever the macro is called.

The final version of the main program in Chapter 4 calls the WriteConsoleA function in three places to output text strings to the command window. All three use five lines of code to provide the arguments in registers RCX, RDX, R8, and R9. The first and last calls are identical, except for the label of the string being displayed. The "msgOut" macro will be built to produce five lines of assembler code from one text line. It will have one parameter: the address (label) of the message to be displayed.

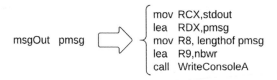

Figure 5.1: Macro expansion example that generates 5 lines of code.

The program in Listing 4.3 is now modified to include the "msgOut" macro and two places where the macro is called. Listing 5.1 shows the entire new main.asm program.

- Lines 10 through 19: Macro msgOut is defined. Notice that it has only one parameter, msg, that will be substituted when the macro is called.
- Line 43: Macro is called to display text beginning at label pmsg.
- Line 63: Macro is called to display text beginning at label newln.

1.		includelib	kernel32.lib	; Windows kernel interface.
2. GetStdHandle	proto			; Function to retrieve I/O handle
3. WriteConsoleA	proto			; Function writes to command window
4. ReadConsoleA	proto			; Function reads from keyboard
5. Console	equ		-11	; Device code for console text output
6. Keyboard	equ		-10	; Device code for console text input
7. MaxBuf	equ		20	; Maximum input buffer size
8. ExitProcess	proto			
9.				
10. ;			Macro "msgOut msg" displays a character string.	
11. ;			msg: Label of ASCII message for command window.	
12.				
13. msgOut	macro		msg	; One argument: msg
14.	mov		RCX,stdout	; Handle to standard output device

```
15.         lea      RDX,msg          ; Pointer to message to display
16.         mov      R8,lengthof msg  ; Number of characters to display
17.         lea      R9,nbwr          ; Number of bytes actually written.
18.         call     WriteConsoleA    ; Write text to command window.
19.         endm
20.
21.         .code
22.
23. ;       Main program that reads text message from user through command
24. ;       window keyin and displays it in same command window.
25. ;               1. Multiple lines input until only "Enter" key pushed.
26. ;               2. Each character input is echoed on a separate line.
27.
28. main    proc
29.
30.         sub      RSP,40           ; Reserve "shadow space" on stack.
31.
32. ;       Obtain "handles" for console I/O streams
33.
34.         mov      RCX,Console      ; Console standard output handle
35.         call     GetStdHandle     ; Returns handle in register RAX
36.         mov      stdout,RAX       ; Save handle of console display.
37.         mov      RCX,Keyboard     ; Console standard input handle
38.         call     GetStdHandle     ; Returns handle in register RAX
39.         mov      stdin,RAX        ; Save handle for keyboard input.
40.
41. ;       Display the prompt message.
42.
43. nxtlin: msgOut   pmsg             ; Write text string to command box.
44.
45. ;       Read input line from user keyboard.
46.
47.         mov      RCX,stdin        ; Handle to standard input device
48.         mov      R8,MaxBuf        ; Maximum length to receive
49.         lea      RDX,keymsg       ; Memory address to receive input
50.         lea      R9,nbrd          ; Number of bytes actually read.
51.         call     ReadConsoleA     ; Read text string from command box.
52.
53. ;       Echo line just input back to the user one character at a time.
54.
55.         lea      R12,keymsg       ; Memory buffer containing input
56.         mov      R13,nbrd         ; Number of characters actually read
57. inloop: mov      RCX,stdout       ; Handle to standard output device
58.         mov      RDX,R12          ; Point to next character to display
59.         mov      R8,1             ; Only display 1 character.
60.         lea      R9,nbwr          ; Number of bytes actually written.
61.         call     WriteConsoleA    ; Write text string to command box.
62.
63.         msgOut   newln            ; Write CR/LF to command box.
```

5: Macros & Subroutines   65

64.	inc	R12	; Set pointer to next character.
65.	dec	R13	; Decrement remaining byte count.
66.	jg	inloop	; Loop until message complete.
67.			
68. ;		Go get another line, but exit if only "Enter" key was input.	
69.			
70.	mov	R8,nbrd	; Length (bytes) of input message
71.	cmp	R8,2	; Test if only CR and LF characters.
72.	jg	nxtlin	; Loop back to get another input.
73.			
74.	add	RSP,40	; Replace "shadow space" on stack
75.	mov	RCX,0	; Set exit status code to zero.
76.	call	ExitProcess	; Return control to Windows.
77.			
78. main	endp		
79.			
80.	.data		
81. pmsg	byte	"Please enter text message: "	
82. keymsg	byte	MaxBuf DUP (?) ; Memory buffer for keyboard input	
83. newln	byte	0DH,0AH	; Carriage return and line feed
84. stdout	qword	?	; Handle to standard output device
85. nbwr	qword	?	; Number of bytes actually written
86. stdin	qword	?	; Handle to standard input device
87. nbrd	qword	?	; Number of bytes actually read
88.			
89.	end		

Listing 5.1: Using a macro to simplify assembler text.

Why didn't I use the msgOut macro for the WriteConsoleA function call on line 61? I could have, but I would have needed a more complicated macro which could handle the different types of message location and size parameters. Instead, I will make a subroutine to handle all three display lines.

Subroutines

A subroutine is a section of code that is "called" to perform a specific job. Depending upon the programming language and application, subroutines are also known as functions, modules, procedures, and methods. Examples of jobs a subroutine can perform:

- Display a number to the user
- Get keyboard input from the user
- Get input from a specific device such as a temperature sensor
- Change the speed of a motor
- Perform a particular type of analysis such as a least-squares fit of data

The program in Listing 5.1 will now be modified by adding a very simple subroutine, v_asc, which will display an ASCII character string in the command window. Listing 5.2 provides the specifications of what v_asc will do and the argument values it needs. Figure 5.2 provides the actual coding.

```
;        Subroutine v_asc displays ASCII string in command window.
;               RDX: Points to first character in memory
;               R8:   Number of bytes to display
;               RSP: 16-byte aligned before CALL
;               RBX,RSI,RDI,RBP,RSP,R12-R15: Contents preserved.
```

Listing 5.2: Subroutine v_asc specifications

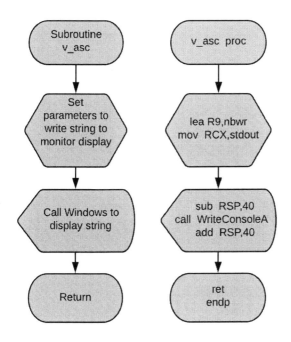

Figure 5.2: Subroutine v_asc displays one character

The first question you might ask: "Since subroutine v_asc is so simple, why bother at all, just use the Windows WriteConsoleA function directly and reduce the additional overhead of a subroutine essentially calling the same type of subroutine." In a very small program with only a few calls, I would agree. However, for larger programs, a dedicated display subroutine provides a lot of flexibility from the maintenance perspective. Just for example, let's say we have developed a program with thousands of calls to WriteConsoleA, and now the "marketplace" requires that we send our display messages to a different device (one that the simple Windows function cannot perform). Wouldn't it be more convenient to accommodate that change in one place in the subroutine's code rather than hunt it down in the large program and try to successfully change it thousands of times?

When the msgOut macro is rewritten to call v_asc instead of WriteConsoleA, it is simpler because subroutine v_asc only has two parameters, not four.

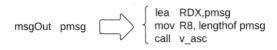

Figure 5.3: Macro expansion calling v_asc.

Listing 5.3 shows the updated main program, including the v_asc subroutine, and calls to the v_asc subroutine:

- Lines 10 through 17: New msgOut macro that calls v_asc.
- Line 57: Call to v_asc to display one character
- Lines 76 through 89: New v_asc subroutine.

```
 1.                    includelib  kernel32.lib    ; Windows kernel interface.
 2. GetStdHandle       proto                       ; Function to retrieve I/O handle
 3. WriteConsoleA      proto                       ; Function writes command window
 4. ReadConsoleA       proto                       ; Function reads from keyboard
 5. Console            equ         -11             ; Device code for console text output
 6. Keyboard           equ         -10             ; Device code for console text input
 7. MaxBuf             equ         20              ; Maximum input buffer size
 8. ExitProcess        proto
 9.
10. ;                  Macro "msgOut msg" displays a character string.
11. ;                              msg:   Label of ASCII message for command window.
12.
13. msgOut             macro       msg             ; One argument: msg
14.                    lea         RDX,msg         ; Pointer to message to display
15.                    mov         R8,lengthof msg ; Number of characters to display
16.                    call        v_asc           ; Write text to command window.
17.                    endm
18.
19.                    .code
20.
21. ;                  Main program that reads text message from user through command
22. ;                  window keyin and displays it in same command window.
23. ;                              1. Multiple lines input until only "Enter" key pushed.
```

```
24. ;                              2. Each character input is echoed on a separate line.
25.
26. main        proc
27.
28.            sub       RSP,40            ; Reserve "shadow space" on stack.
29.
30. ;          Obtain "handles" for console I/O streams
31.
32.            mov       RCX,Console       ; Console standard output handle
33.            call      GetStdHandle      ; Returns handle in register RAX
34.            mov       stdout,RAX        ; Save handle of console display.
35.            mov       RCX,Keyboard      ; Console standard input handle
36.            call      GetStdHandle      ; Returns handle in register RAX
37.            mov       stdin,RAX         ; Save handle for keyboard input.
38.
39. ;          Display the prompt message.
40.
41. nxtlin:    msgOut    pmsg              ; Write text string to command box.
42.
43. ;          Read input line from user keyboard.
44.
45.            mov       RCX,stdin         ; Handle to standard input device
46.            mov       R8,MaxBuf         ; Maximum length to receive
47.            lea       RDX,keymsg        ; Memory address to receive input
48.            lea       R9,nbrd           ; Number of bytes actually read.
49.            call      ReadConsoleA      ; Read text string from keyboard.
50.
51. ;          Echo line just input back to the user one character at a time.
52.
53.            lea       R12,keymsg        ; Memory buffer containing input
54.            mov       R13,nbrd          ; Number of characters actually read
55. inloop:    mov       RDX,R12           ; Point to next character to display
56.            mov       RCX,1             ; Only display 1 character.
57.            call      v_asc             ; Write text string to command box.
58.
59.            msgOut    newln             ; Write CR/LF to command box.
60.            inc       R12               ; Set pointer to next character.
61.            dec       R13               ; Decrement remaining byte count.
62.            jg        inloop            ; Loop until message complete.
63.
64. ;          Go get another line, but exit if only "Enter" key was input.
65.
66.            mov       R8,nbrd           ; Length (bytes) of input message
67.            cmp       R8,2              ; Test if only CR and LF characters.
68.            jg        nxtlin            ; Loop back around for more input.
69.
70.            add       RSP,40            ; Replace "shadow space" on stack.
71.            mov       RCX,0             ; Set exit status code to zero.
72.            call      ExitProcess       ; Return control to Windows.
```

```
73.
74. main          endp
75.
76. ;             Subroutine v_asc displays ASCII string in command window.
77. ;                       RDX: Points to first character in memory
78. ;                       R8:  Number of bytes to display
79. ;                       RSP: 16-byte aligned before CALL
80. ;                       RBX,RSI,RDI,RBP,RSP,R12-R15: Preserved.
81.
82. v_asc         proc
83.               lea     R9,nbwr           ; Number of bytes actually written.
84.               mov     RCX,stdout        ; Handle to standard output device
85.               sub     RSP,40            ; Reserve "shadow space" on stack.
86.               call    WriteConsoleA     ; Write text string to command box.
87.               add     RSP,40            ; Replace "shadow space" on stack
88.               ret                       ; Return to the calling program.
89. v_asc         endp
90.
91.               .data
92. pmsg          byte    "Please enter text message: "
93. keymsg        byte    MaxBuf DUP (?) ; Memory buffer for keyboard input
94. newln         byte    0DH,0AH           ; Carriage return and line feed
95. stdout        qword   ?                 ; Handle to standard output device
96. nbwr          qword   ?                 ; Number of bytes actually written
97. stdin         qword   ?                 ; Handle to standard input device
98. nbrd          qword   ?                 ; Number of bytes actually read
99.
100.              end
```

Listing 5.3: Main program with subroutine v_asc

The advantages of using subroutines are many:

- Subroutines help organize the construction of the program.
- The code only takes up memory space once.
- It's less work to modify or correct one area of common code rather than many copies of almost identical code.
- "Information hiding" occurs because one part of the program is unable to directly access data in another part of the program and accidentally change it.
- Division of programming assignments is easier.

The disadvantages of subroutines are few.

- There is a slight performance degradation compared to "in-line code" due to the overhead of the call and return.
- It can lead to too much of a good thing: Too many tiny subroutines can lead to confusion.

X64 Calling Convention

Assembly language programs that either call the Windows API functions or are a part of a C or C++ program must abide by the X64 Calling Convention. As described in Chapter 3, the X64 Calling Convention declares which registers contain the arguments, which registers' contents will be preserved, and the 16-byte RSP alignment requirement.

A "leaf" function or subroutine is one that does not call another subroutine or function. It, therefore does not have to be as concerned about the calling convention as other subroutines. Since it calls no subroutines, no other subroutine will destroy its register contents, and it doesn't have to be concerned about the RSP 16-byte alignment unless it uses AVX aligned instructions. It does have to protect the non-volatile register contents for the program that called it.

The X64 Calling Convention also describes floating point values passed in XMM registers for use in SSE instructions. Appendix D and Chapters 11 and 12 provide those details.

LEA or OFFSET

I have used the LEA instruction to load the effective address of variables in memory. The OFFSET assembly language directive along with a MOV instruction can do the same thing, and even a little faster in most cases. However, the LEA instruction is more flexible and can work with addresses in registers as well. Figure 5.4 shows macro msgOut implemented with the offset directive.

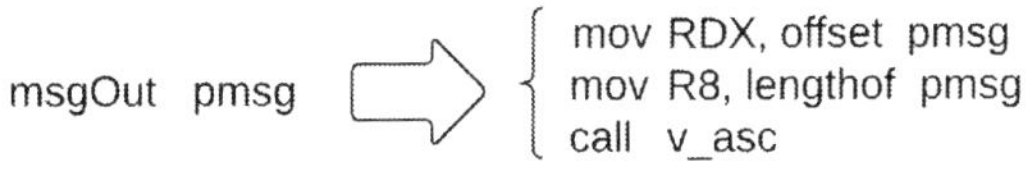

```
msgOut  pmsg   ⇒   { mov RDX, offset  pmsg
                     mov R8, lengthof  pmsg
                     call  v_asc
```

Figure 5.4: Macro msgOut using offset assembly-time function.

From a user's perspective, both programs in this chapter (Listings 5.1 and 5.3) appear to run exactly the same as the main.asm program in Chapter 4. They echo a text line one character per line. Go ahead and compile, link, and execute the programs in Listings 5.1 and 5.3 as you did in Chapter 4 and verify that they behave the same. The techniques discussed in this chapter are recommended for better program development and maintenance.

Review Questions

1. What is a "leaf" function or subroutine?
2. * How is a macro different from a subroutine?
3. * Give an example of a useful macro that generates neither any instructions nor any data.
4. * What is a principal danger in using "pass by reference"?
5. Within the X64 Calling Convention, which registers can be changed by a subroutine and not be restored to their original values before returning?
6. List the locations for the first four arguments in calling a subroutine according to the X64 Calling Convention?
7. Within the X64 Calling Convention, the first four arguments are in registers and any additional arguments are on the run-time stack (RSP register). Provide a MOV instruction that would load the fifth argument into register R15.

Programming Exercises

1. Temporarily modify the v_asc subroutine so that it is 100% X64 Calling Convention compatible. Note: The location of the arguments will have to be changed.
2. Change each of the LEA instructions in Listing 5.3 to a MOV instruction with OFFSET assembler directive. Recompile and run the program to verify that the results are identical.

— 6 —
Link & LIB

We have been overlooking the middle step of the compile-link-execute sequence. By not having the compile-only /c option on the ML64 command, the assembler has been invoking the linker for us by default. In Chapter 6, we will break out the v_asc subroutine into its own source file, and then link its object module with the main program's object module, both in separate files. We will also build an object code library using the LIB command and examine it with the DUMPBIN utility.

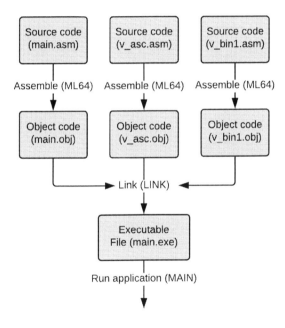

Figure 6.1: Dividing a program into modules

Figure 6.1 shows where we're heading: The main program will be in a source file by itself, and each of the display subroutines will be in separate files. We will first split the program from Listing 5.3 into two source files by isolating subroutine v_asc to its own file. Then in the next couple of chapters, we will built new source files containing subroutines v_bin1 for binary, v_hex1 for hexadecimal, and v_dig1 for decimal display. The link command will bring them all together along with the API functions in kernel32.lib to make a working program.

We begin by putting subroutine v_asc into a file all by itself, but it is somewhat more complicated because v_asc needs the handle ID number from the GetStdHandle for the command window display. This separation can be programmed several ways. For example, I could still get the handle in the main program and pass it to v_asc as another argument. There is some merit to that approach, but a better way is to make a new v_opn subroutine that is in the same source file as v_asc. If this were a large application with thousands of calls to display text, this latter approach offers flexibility of migrating to a whole different type of display environment.

As I hinted above, I will be adding more individual subroutines to display just one character, or byte, in binary, hexadecimal, and decimal formats. For consistency, I will also make a new subroutine that is specialized to display only one byte in ASCII. Listing 6.1 shows the new v_asc.asm file containing three subroutines: v_opn, v_asc, and v_asc1.

- Lines 6 through 9: Subroutine v_asc needs the Windows API functions that formerly appeared in the main program.
- Lines 12 through 22: Subroutine v_opn obtains the handle needed by v_asc and v_asc1.
- Lines 24 through 37: Subroutine v_asc is same as before, but now in its own source file.
- Lines 39 through 53: New subroutine v_asc1 displays only 1 character.
- Lines 56 and 57: Local storage for variables associated with WriteConsoleA.

1. ;			Subroutines to display one or more characters on the console.
2. ;			v_opn: Opens the standard display monitor
3. ;			v_asc: Displays string of characters in memory buffer
4. ;			v_asc1: Displays one characters in memory buffer
5.			
6.	includelib	kernel32.lib	; Windows kernel interface.
7. GetStdHandle	proto		; Function to retrieve I/O handle
8. WriteConsoleA	proto		; Function writes command window
9. Console	equ	-11	; Device code for console text output
10.	.code		
11.			
12. ;			Subroutine v_opn will open the standard display monitor.
13. ;			RBX,RSI,RDI,RBP,RSP,R12-R15: Preserved.
14.			
15. v_opn	proc		
16.	mov	RCX,Console	; Console standard output handle
17.	sub	RSP,40	; Reserve "shadow space" on stack.
18.	call	GetStdHandle	; Returns handle in register RAX

```
19.             add     RSP,40          ; Replace "shadow space" on stack
20.             mov     stdout,RAX      ; Save handle of console display.
21.             ret                     ; Return to the calling program.
22. v_opn       endp
23.
24. ;          Subroutine v_asc displays ASCII string in command window.
25. ;                      RDX: Points to first character in memory
26. ;                      R8:  Number of bytes to display
27. ;                      RSP: 16-byte aligned before CALL
28. ;                      RBX,RSI,RDI,RBP,RSP,R12-R15: Preserved.
29.
30. v_asc       proc
31.             lea     R9,nbwr         ; Number of bytes actually written.
32.             mov     RCX,stdout      ; Handle to standard output device
33.             sub     RSP,40          ; Reserve "shadow space" on stack.
34.             call    WriteConsoleA   ; Write text string to command box.
35.             add     RSP,40          ; Replace "shadow space" on stack
36.             ret                     ; Return to the calling program.
37. v_asc       endp
38.
39. ;          Subroutine v_asc1 will display 1 character in memory buffer.
40. ;                      R12: Points to the one character in memory
41. ;                      RSP: 16-byte aligned before CALL
42. ;                      Registers preserved: RBX,RBP,RDI,RSI,RSP,R12-R15
43.
44. v_asc1      proc
45.             mov     R8,1            ; Number of bytes requested to write.
46.             lea     R9,nbwr         ; Number of bytes actually written.
47.             mov     RDX,R12         ; Memory address of buffer to write
48.             mov     RCX,stdout      ; I/O handle for display monitor.
49.             sub     RSP,40          ; Reserve "shadow space" on stack.
50.             call    WriteConsoleA   ; Write text string to command box.
51.             add     RSP,40          ; Replace "shadow space" on stack
52.             ret                     ; Return to the calling program.
53. v_asc1      endp
54.
55.             .data
56. stdout      qword   ?               ; Handle to standard output device
57. nbwr        qword   ?               ; Number of bytes actually written
58.             end
```

Listing 6.1: Subroutines v_asc, v_asc1, and v_opn

Subroutine v_asc1 displays one character in ASCII. Of course, v_asc1 could have been programmed so that it calls v_asc to output the one character rather than going straight to WriteConsoleA. If it was a more complicated situation or if both subroutines were not in the same source code file, I probably would have done that. Instead, I programmed it as shown in Figure 6.2.

6: Link & LIB

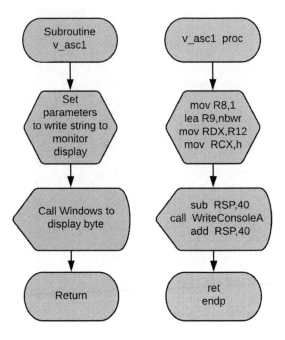

Figure 6.2: Subroutine v_asc1 displays one character

Listing 6.2 shows the updated main program which now calls v_opn and v_asc1:

- Lines 7 through 9: The prototypes for subroutines v_asc, v_asc1, and v_opn, which are now external to the main source code file and therefore must now be declared. Note that the prototype for WriteConsoleA is no longer needed here.
- Line 33: Subroutine v_opn will get the handle that will be used by subroutines v_asc and v_asc1..
- Line 54: Subroutine v_asc1 is more specialized than v_asc, and it needs fewer arguments.

1.		includelib	kernel32.lib	; Windows kernel interface.
2. GetStdHandle	proto			; Function to retrieve I/O handles
3. ReadConsoleA	proto			; Function reads keyboard buffer
4. Keyboard	equ		-10	; Device code for console text input.
5. MaxBuf	equ		20	; Maximum input buffer size
6. ExitProcess	proto			
7. v_asc	proto			; Function writes ASCII string.
8. v_asc1	proto			; Function writes one ASCII character.
9. v_opn	proto			; Function opens display stream.

```
10.
11. ;                     Macro "msgOut msg" calls subroutine to display a string.
12. ;                         msg:   Label of ASCII message for command window.
13.
14. msgOut       macro       msg              ; One argument: msg
15.              lea         RDX,msg          ; Pointer to message to display
16.              mov         R8,lengthof msg  ; Number of characters to display
17.              call        v_asc            ; Write text to command window.
18.              endm
19.
20.              .code
21.
22. ;                     Main program that reads text message from user through command
23. ;                     window keyin and displays it in same command window.
24. ;                             1. Multiple lines are input until only "Enter" key pushed.
25. ;                             2. Each character input will be echoed on a separate line.
26.
27. main         proc
28.
29.              sub         RSP,40           ; Reserve "shadow space" on stack.
30.
31. ;                     Obtain "handles" for console Input/Output streams
32.
33.              call        v_opn            ; Open text display stream.
34.              mov         RCX,Keyboard     ; Console standard input handle
35.              call        GetStdHandle     ; Returns handle in register RAX
36.              mov         stdin,RAX        ; Save handle for keyboard input.
37.
38. ;                     Display the prompt message.
39.
40. nxtlin:      msgOut      pmsg             ; Write text string to command box.
41.
42. ;                     Read input line from user keyboard.
43.
44.              mov         RCX,stdin        ; Handle to standard input device
45.              mov         R8,MaxBuf        ; Maximum length to receive
46.              lea         RDX,keymsg       ; Memory address to receive input
47.              lea         R9,nbrd          ; Number of bytes actually read.
48.              call        ReadConsoleA     ; Read text string from command box.
49.
50. ;                     Echo line just input back to the user one character at a time.
51.
52.              lea         R12,keymsg       ; Memory buffer containing input
53.              mov         R13,nbrd         ; Number of characters actually read
54. inloop:      call        v_asc1           ; Display one ASCII character
55.              msgOut      newln            ; Output carriage return / line feed
56.              inc         R12              ; Set pointer to next character.
57.              dec         R13              ; Decrement bytes remaining.
58.              jg          inloop           ; Loop until message complete.
```

59.			
60. ;		Go get another line, but exit if only "Enter" key was input.	
61.			
62.	mov	R8,nbrd	; Length (bytes) of input message
63.	cmp	R8,2	; Test if only CR and LF characters.
64.	jg	nxtlin	; Loop back for more input.
65.			
66.	add	RSP,40	; Replace "shadow space" on stack
67.	mov	RCX,0	; Set exit status code to zero.
68.	call	ExitProcess	; Return control to Windows.
69. main	endp		
70.			
71.	.data		
72. stdin	qword	?	; Handle to standard input device
73. nbrd	qword	?	; Number of bytes actually read
74. pmsg	byte	"Please enter text message: "	
75. keymsg	byte	MaxBuf DUP (?) ; Memory buffer for keyboard input	
76. newln	byte	0DH,0AH	; Carriage return and line feed
77.	end		

Listing 6.2: Main program calling v_asc1

Listing 6.3 shows that the sequence of commands to compile-link-execute are the same as before except the ML64 line now has both main.asm and v_asc.asm (separated by a blank) instead of only main.asm. This approach works fine for compiling and linking a few files. It will be used in some of the following chapters as well. However, as the number of object files increases, building a library is more practical.

```
C:\ASM64> path  C:\######\Hostx64\x64;%PATH%
C:\ASM64> copy  X64_Asm-master\Listing_6_1.txt  v_asc.asm
1 file(s) copied.
C:\ASM64> copy  X64_Asm-master\Listing_6_2.txt  main.asm
1 file(s) copied.
C:\ASM64> ML64 main.asm v_asc.asm /link /SUBSYSTEM:CONSOLE /ENTRY:main
Microsoft (R) Macro Assembler (x64) Version 14.11.25547.0
Copyright (C) Microsoft Corporation. All rights reserved.

Assembling: main.asm
Assembling: v_asc.asm
Microsoft (R) Incremental Linker Version 14.11.25547.0
Copyright (C) Microsoft Corporation. All rights reserved.

/OUT:main.exe
main.obj
v_asc.obj
/SUBSYSTEM:CONSOLE
/ENTRY:main
```

```
C:\ASM64>main
Please enter text message: Hi
H
i


Please enter text message:


C:\ASM64>
```

Listing 6.3: Compile and link with two source code files

Although assembly and linking with one command line is convenient for a very small program, the following separate command steps lead to more versatility.

- ML64   /c   main.asm   v_asc.asm
- LINK   /out:main.exe   main.obj   v_asc.obj   /entry:main

LIB and DUMPBIN

The kernel32.lib file contains hundreds of entry points to the Windows API functions. A user library file can also be constructed and is very convenient as the number of subroutines grow. The main program will need a second includelib line as shown below for a library named user.lib (it could be any name such as x.lib).

1. includelib   kernel32.lib   ; Windows kernel interface.
2. includelib   user.lib   ; Contains v_opn, v_asc, and v_asc1.

The user.lib file can be built and accessed by the main program using the following three lines.

1. ML64   /c   v_asc.asm
2. LIB   /out : user.lib   /verbose   v_asc.obj
3. ML64   main.asm   /link   /SUBSYSTEM : CONSOLE   /ENTRY : main

The first line assembles source code v_asc.asm into object file v_asc.obj. In the second line, the library is created with only the one object file, and the third line will build the absolute as before. The end of Chapter 7 has a further example of building and using a library where four object files are involved.

The DUMPBIN program provides some interesting internal information on a variety of file types. Enter "DUMPBIN   /symbols   user.lib" from the command line to get a list of global names used by the linker.

Review Questions

1. What are two advantage of breaking a program into multiple source files?
2. What is a disadvantage (i.e., how much extra work is required) of building a program from multiple source code files?
3. * If you were going to build a library named "engines.lib" from three object files named "electric.obj," "gasoline.obj," and "diesel.obj," what command line would be needed?
4. * What assembler directive would be used to find the "engines.lib" library built in question 3?

Programming Exercises

1. Write subroutine v_asc1 so that it calls v_asc rather than WriteConsoleA.
2. Use DUMPBIN on v_asc.asm and v_asc.obj to see what details it provides.

— 7 —

Binary & Hexadecimal

What's wrong with decimal? Babbage's Analytical Engine computer design was decimal. Have we digressed in the past 200 years? Actually, there have been many decimal-based computers, but why are almost all of today's computers based on binary? The simple answer is that the logical building blocks (i.e., electronics in today's systems) are simpler and more efficient in binary than they are in decimal. The importance of hexadecimal in computer applications is that it's a compact form of binary.

In Chapter 7, the main console program from the previous chapters will be modified to echo the input text line as single characters in ASCII, binary, and hexadecimal. Shift, logical, and string instructions using byte registers will be demonstrated in the example programs.

Introductions

X86-64 instructions appearing for the first time in Chapter 7:

- PUSH: Saves the contents of a 64-bit register on the stack and then decrements the RSP stack pointer by 8. Chapter 3 described stack operations, but the PUSH instruction has not been demonstrated until this chapter.
- POP: Reverses the PUSH instruction by loading the 8 bytes from the top of the stack into a 64-bit register. The RSP stack pointer will be incremented by 8.
- SHR: Shift data bits in a register to the right, and zero fill "empty" bit positions on left (logical shift).
- AND: Bit-by-bit Boolean logic "and" operation
- STOSB: Store contents of register AL into next position in string pointed to by register RDI.
- CLD (CLear the Direction flag): Sets the direction for auto-incrementation of register RDI (used by STOSB).
- XLAT: Translate the value in register AL to a new value from table pointed to by register RBX.

Binary Display

A decimal number is really a short notation for a polynomial of powers of 10. For example: 137 is $1 \times 10^2 + 3 \times 10^1 + 7 \times 10^0$. Likewise, a binary number is really a short notation for a polynomial of powers of 2. For example: 110101 is $1{\times}2^5 + 1{\times}2^4 + 0{\times}2^3 + 1{\times}2^2 + 0{\times}2^1 + 1{\times}2^0$. By the way, this polynomial structure is the main reason we count bits from right to left starting with zero. For a more thorough description of the ASCII code and binary, please see Appendices F and G, respectively.

A character code is a set that assigns a unique number to each text character. For example in both the ASCII and Unicode sets, the letter "A" is assigned the value 65 (which is hexadecimal 41 and binary 01000001). A new subroutine, v_bin1, will be programmed to display a character as a series of 8 binary digits (bits), and that subroutine will be called by the main program for display.

Subroutine v_bin1 can be programmed many different ways, but I will program it using a loop that counts down from 7 to 0 and demonstrate the use of byte registers, string instructions, register shifts, and logical instructions.

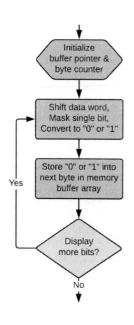

Figure 7.1: Program loop to display 8 bits

Instructions in the loop select a particular bit, convert it to an ASCII "0" or "1" character, and store it into a memory buffer. Subroutine v_asc will then be called to display all eight characters at once.

1. Preparation: Initialize "count down" byte register CL to 7. CL also identifies the first bit in the data (loaded into byte register DL).

2. A process to be repeated multiple times: Select the next bit, indicated by value in CL, and convert it to either an ASCII "0" or "1" character.

3. Decision when to exit the loop: Register CL is decremented by one on each pass through the loop which allows it to point to all bit positions 7 through 0. When CL is decremented from 0 to -1, then an exit from the loop is taken because all 8 bit positions have been displayed.

Bit Shift Operations

Almost all CPU architectures include several instructions for shifting bits within a register. Most CPU architectures support three types of shifts:

- Logical: Bits shifted out from either end of the register are discarded and new zero bits fill in on the opposite side.
- Circular (also referred to as rotate): Bits shifted out one end of the register come back in on the other side.
- Arithmetic: This is similar to a logical right shift except arithmetic shift brings in copies of the sign bit instead of zero.

Logical shifts have many applications. One common application is converting between serial and parallel, and a second is for multiplying an integer by a power of two. For example, a one bit shift to the left is multiplying by two, while a two bit shift is multiplying by four. Some computers shift only one bit at a time. In the X86-64, multiple bit shifts can be indicated either from the contents of the CL register or an immediate value in the instruction.

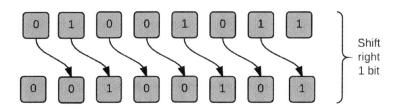

Figure 7.2: Logical right shift moves out bit on right and brings in zero on left.

A shift to the right is like dividing by a power of two, but be aware of two basic problems. Division can have a remainder which will get truncated, not rounded. Secondly, there are two problems with negative integers. A logical right shift will bring in a zero in bit 63, thereby converting a negative number to an inappropriate positive number. The arithmetic shift will solve the negative problem, but a rounding error is still present, so be careful using shifts to divide negative numbers. Please see Appendix G if you need an explanation why the high-order bit (bit 63) is a "1" for negative 64-bit numbers. A circular shift, also referred to as a rotate, allows the bits to be shifted without losing anything out one end or the other.

Logical Operations

The X86-64 processors provide the Boolean AND, inclusive OR, and exclusive OR logical operations. The AND will be used here in Chapter 7, while examples using the two OR operations will appear in Chapter 10.

AND

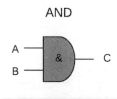

A	B	C = A & B
0	0	0
0	1	0
1	0	0
1	1	1

Figure 7.3: AND operation truth table

The truth table in Figure 7.3 gives the four possible outputs for an AND operation having two inputs.

1. If inputs A and B are both 0, the output will be 0.
2. If A is 0 and B is 1, the output will be 0.
3. If A is 1 and B is 0, the output will be 0.
4. Only if both A and B are 1 will the output be 1.

In the loop in subroutine v_bin1, the AND instruction will remove all data bits except for the bit position currently being examined.

The logical instructions in almost all CPUs are "bitwise" logical operations:

- In the 64-bit X86-64 registers, sixty-four logical operations are performed in parallel. Figure 7.4 only shows a portion of the 64 pairs of corresponding bits being ANDed together.
- Figure 7.4 illustrates the AND instruction. The inclusive OR and exclusive OR (XOR) are also bitwise instructions using 64 pairs of bits, and they will be demonstrated in Chapter 10.

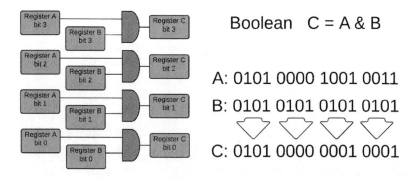

Figure 7.4: Examples of "bitwise" AND of two values

Table 7.1 provides an example where eight passes through a loop select each bit from 01010100B (letter T in ASCII) as CL is decremented from 7 to 0. Figure 7.5 illustrates the combination of the SHR and AND instructions to select the bit from position 3 and put it into bit position 0 all by itself.

CL	SHR AL,CL	AND AL,1
7	00000000	0
6	00000001	1
5	00000010	0
4	00000101	1
3	00001010	0
2	00010101	1
1	00101010	0
0	01010100	0

Table 7.1: SHR and AND instructions select 8 bits of ASCII T to be displayed

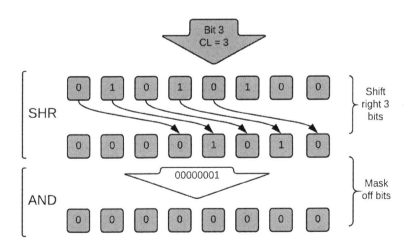

Figure 7.5: Isolate desired bit using SHR and AND instructions.

Byte, Word, Double, and Quad Word Registers

The low-order (right side) byte, word, and double word of each 64-bit general purpose register can be used as individual registers themselves. Table 7.2 provides these register names that are available in the X86-64 architecture.

64-bit registers	32-bit registers	16-bit registers	8-bit registers
RAX	EAX	AX	AL
RBX	EBX	BX	BL
RCX	ECX	CX	CL
RDX	EDX	DX	DL
RSI	ESI	SI	SIL
RDI	EDI	DI	DIL
RBP	EBP	BP	BPL
RSP	ESP	SP	SPL
R8	R8D	R8W	R8B
R9	R9D	R9W	R9B
R10	R10D	R10W	R10B
R11	R11D	R11W	R11B
R12	R12D	R12W	R12B
R13	R13D	R13W	R13B
R14	R14D	R14W	R14B
R15	R15D	R15W	R15B

Table 7.2: X86-64 general purpose integer registers and "fractions"

Notes regarding the use of the above registers:

- The list of above register names work with the Microsoft ML64 assembler. Other documentation, such as that from Intel, have named eight of the 8-bit registers as R8L through R15L instead of R8B through R15B.
- Loading the 8, 16, and 32 bit fractions generally do not affect other bits in the 64-bit register. For example: Moving a value into R15B does not affect bits 8 through 63 in register R15. However, there are special move instructions that either zero fill (MOVZX) or sign extend (MOVSX) to fill the upper bits.
- Registers SIL, DIL, BPL, and SPL did not exist in the 8086 because

the SI, DI, BP, and SP registers were only used as pointers into memory segments and were not general purpose at that time.

- Segment registers from the 8086 (such as DS and ES) are not listed above or described in this book because they have not been extended to be 64-bit general purpose registers.

Four additional byte registers from the original Intel 8086 are also available in the X86-64 architecture. Registers AH, BH, CH, and DH, which consist of bits 8 through 15 in registers RAX, RBX, RCX, and RDX, respectively, are for compatibility with instructions available in the 8086 and can only be used with other 8-bit registers from the 8086. For example: MOV AH,R8L is not a legal X86-64 instruction. As an example, Figure 7.6 shows register names by which fractions of general purpose register RCX can be accessed directly in instructions.

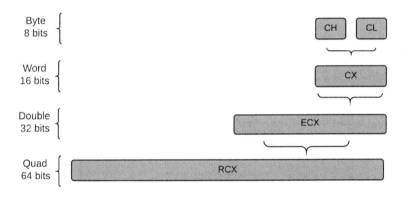

Figure 7.6: Dividing general purpose register RCX into byte, word, and double word components

Loop Through 8 Binary Digits (Bits)

The specifications for using subroutine v_bin1 are the following:

1. The subroutine name is v_bin1, and it's purpose is to display one 8-bit value.
2. The byte to be displayed is passed by reference in register R12 (i.e., R12 points to it in memory).
3. The RSP contains the return address from a call instruction, and it was 128-bit aligned before the call.
4. The calling program can assume that the contents of registers RBX, RBP, RSI, RDI, RSP, and R12-R15 are preserved (i.e., same as the the non-volatile set of registers in the X64 Calling Convention). The other registers are volatile.

The above information is all that a calling program needs to know about subroutine v_bin1. It does not need to know how v_bin1 works internally, but we do since we are examining the code. I have programmed v_bin1 to loop through 8 bits, convert them to a string of eight ASCII characters ("1" and "0") in memory, and then call v_asc to display the string. I use 8-bit "byte" registers along with special logical and shift instructions and string manipulation instructions.

How does subroutine v_bin1 work? We build a loop which counts down from 7 (the position of the leftmost bit) to 0 (the position of the rightmost bit). Register CL not only counts down from 7 to 0, but also indicates which bit is examined on each pass through the loop.

Listing 7.1 shows the entire v_bin1.asm subroutine that will be assembled and then linked with the main and v_asc files.

- Line 5: Subroutine v_bin1 will be calling subroutine v_asc.
- Line 8: This instruction not only preserves the contents of non-volatile register RDI, but it also adjusts the RSP stack pointer to maintain the 16-byte alignment when v_asc is called on line 28 (both are requirements of the X64 Calling Convention).
- Line 9: Register DL (lower 8 bits of RDX) is loaded with the contents of one byte in memory pointed to by register R12. The other bits in RDX are unaffected, but it would not matter if they were as far as subroutine v_bin1 is concerned.
- Line 10: Register RDI (used in upcoming STOSB instruction on line 20) is initialized to the address of memory buffer to be filled.
- Line 11: String instructions, such as STOSB, either automatically increment or decrement the index register (RDI) pointing to the next memory location for data storage. If the direction flag is 0 (i.e., cleared by the CLD instruction), then STOB will automatically add 1 to RDI after the byte has been stored.
- Line 12: Register CL will both identify the next bit to display as well as count down each pass through the loop.
- Lines 14 through 22: Each pass through the loop selects a particular bit by shifting, masking, and then storing either an ASCII "0" or "1" in next position in memory.
- Lines 16,17: The next bit is moved into the low order (rightmost) bit position in register AL all by itself.
- Line 20: Stores contents of register AL into memory location pointed to by register RDI and then increments RDI by 1. If the "direction flag" was set (STD instruction instead of CLD on line 11), then RDI would have been decremented.
- Lines 21,22: The value 1 is subtracted from the contents of byte register CL, and the loop continues until CL is decremented to -1.
- Line 30: "Pop" both restores the contents of non-volatile register RDI and the RSP stack pointer.

```
1. ;            Subroutine v_bin1 displays one byte from memory in binary.
2. ;                    R12: Points to the byte in memory
3. ;                    Registers preserved: RBX,RBP,RDI,RSI,RSP,R12-R15
4.
5. v_asc    proto                  ; Declare external subroutine.
6.         .code
7. v_bin1   proc                   ; Subroutine v_bin1 entry point
8.         push    RDI            ; Save RDI and decrement RSP by 8
9.         mov     DL,[R12]       ; Load byte to be displayed
10.        lea     RDI,bits8      ; Pointer to ASCII display buffer
11.        cld                    ; String instructions will increment.
12.        mov     CL,7           ; Bit 7 will be output first.
13.
14. ;            Loop through bits 7 to 0 converting them to ASCII.
15.
16. nxtbit:  mov     AL,DL          ; Copy byte to be displayed to AL.
17.        shr     AL,CL          ; Shift current bit to bit 0.
18.        and     AL,1           ; Mask off all bits except bit 0.
19.        add     AL,'0'         ; Map binary 0,1 to ASCII '0','1'
20.        stosb                  ; Store in array of 8 "bits."
21.        dec     CL             ; Number of bits left to process.
22.        jge     nxtbit         ; Continue until all 8 bits done.
23. ;
24. ;            Display all 8 bits of current byte from memory buffer.
25. ;
26.        lea     RDX,bits8      ; Points to 8-byte memory buffer
27.        mov     R8,8           ; Number of characters to display
28.        call    v_asc          ; Subroutine that displays ASCII
29.
30.        pop     RDI            ; Reload RDI and reposition stack
31.        ret                    ; Return to the calling program
32. v_bin1   endp
33.
34.        .data
35. bits8    byte    8 DUP (?)      ; Memory buffer for display
36.        end
```

Listing 7.1: Subroutine v_bin1 displays a binary number in ASCII

Special purpose registers for string instructions:

- AL: Register assumed to be used in string instructions. Similar examples using registers AX, EAX, and RAX appear in Chapter 9.
- RSI: Source Index of next byte to load into register AL using string instructions.
- RDI: Destination Index of next byte to store from register AL.

- CL: Count of number of bits to shift. Register RCL can also be used as a count down to zero register with LOOP instructions.

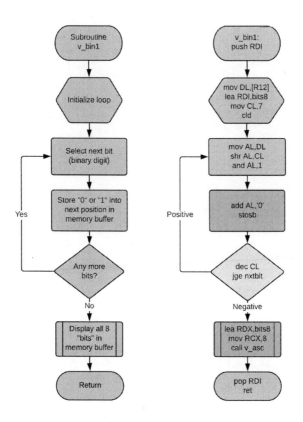

Figure 7.7: Subroutine v_bin1 design

Main Program

The main program will now be modified to call v_bin1 in addition to v_asc1 so that each character input will be echoed in both binary and ASCII. Later in this chapter, a third subroutine v_hex1 will be called, thereby providing hexadecimal, binary, and ASCII for each character input.

Each of the subroutines, v_asc1, v_bin1, and v_hex1, will be called followed by a separation character such as a tab. Macro "disp" will be created to call a subroutine and then write out a separation character. As show in Figure 7.8, macro disp is a simple macro with two arguments: subroutine name and address of separation character(s) in memory. It is a simple macro, but it does demonstrate nesting macros, where one macro calls another.

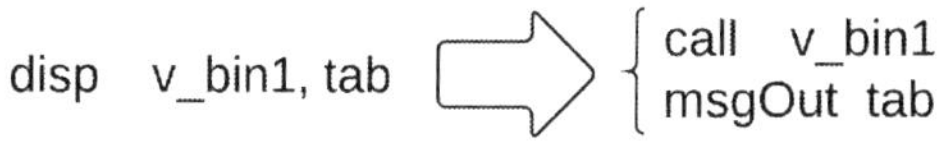

disp   v_bin1, tab   ⟹   { call   v_bin1
                             { msgOut tab

Figure 7.8: Macro expansion generates another macro to be expanded.

The main program in Listing 7.2 includes the following changes for calling v_bin1 and using the new macro:

- Line 10: Declare external subroutine v_bin1.
- Lines 21 through 28: Definition of new "disp" macro.

1.	includelib	kernel32.lib	; Windows kernel interface.
2. GetStdHandle	proto		; Function to retrieve I/O handles
3. ReadConsoleA	proto		; Function reads keyboard buffer
4. Keyboard	equ	-10	; Device code for console text input.
5. MaxBuf	equ	20	; Maximum input buffer size
6. ExitProcess	proto		
7. v_asc	proto		; Function writes ASCII string.
8. v_asc1	proto		; Function writes one ASCII character.
9. v_opn	proto		; Function opens display stream.
10. v_bin1	proto		; Display byte in binary
11.			
12. ;		Macro "msgOut msg" calls subroutine to display a string.
13. ;		msg: Label of ASCII message for command window.
14.			
15. msgOut	macro	msg	; One argument: msg
16.	lea	RDX,msg	; Pointer to message to display
17.	mov	R8,lengthof msg	; Number of characters to display
18.	call	v_asc	; Write text to command window.
19.	endm		
20.			
21. ;		Macro "disp sub,tail" calls a subroutine, then displays a character.
22. ;		sub: Subroutine to be called
23. ;		tail: Separation character string to be output
24.			
25. disp	macro	sub,tail	; Two arguments
26.	call	sub	; Subroutine to display a byte
27.	msgOut	tail	; String of separation characters
28.	endm		
29.			
30.	.code		
31.			
32. ;		Main program that reads text message from user through command
33. ;		window keyin and displays it in same command window.

```
34. ;                        1. Multiple lines are input until only "Enter" key pushed.
35. ;                        2. Each character input will be echoed on a separate line.
36.
37. main        proc
38.
39.            sub       RSP,40          ; Reserve "shadow space" on stack.
40.
41. ;          Obtain "handles" for console Input streams
42.
43.            call      v_opn           ; Open text display stream.
44.            mov       RCX,Keyboard    ; Console standard input handle
45.            call      GetStdHandle    ; Returns handle in register RAX
46.            mov       stdin,RAX       ; Save handle for keyboard input.
47.
48. ;          Display the prompt message.
49.
50. nxtlin:    msgOut    pmsg            ; Write text string to command box.
51.
52. ;          Read input line from user keyboard.
53.
54.            mov       RCX,stdin       ; Handle to standard input device
55.            mov       R8,MaxBuf       ; Maximum length to receive
56.            lea       RDX,keymsg      ; Memory address to receive input
57.            lea       R9,nbrd         ; Number of bytes actually read.
58.            call      ReadConsoleA    ; Read text string from command box.
59.
60. ;          Echo line just input back to the user one character at a time.
61.
62.            lea       R12,keymsg      ; Memory buffer containing input
63.            mov       R13,nbrd        ; Number of characters actually read
64. inloop:    disp      v_bin1,tab      ; Display byte as 8 bits.
65.            disp      v_asc1,newln    ; Display byte as ASCII character.
66.            inc       R12             ; Set pointer to next character.
67.            dec       R13             ; Decrement bytes remaining.
68.            jg        inloop          ; Loop until message complete.
69.
70. ;          Go get another line, but exit if only "Enter" key was input.
71.
72.            mov       R8,nbrd         ; Length (bytes) of input message
73.            cmp       R8,2            ; Test if only CR and LF characters.
74.            jg        nxtlin          ; Loop back for more input.
75.
76.            add       RSP,40          ; Replace "shadow space" on stack
77.            mov       RCX,0           ; Set exit status code to zero.
78.            call      ExitProcess     ; Return control to Windows.
79.
80. main       endp
81.
82.            .data
```

83. pmsg	byte	"Please enter text message: "
84. keymsg	byte	MaxBuf DUP (?) ; Memory buffer for keyboard input
85. newln	byte	0DH,0AH ; Carriage return and line feed
86. tab	byte	09H ; Horizontal tab character
87. stdin	qword	? ; Handle to standard input device
88. nbrd	qword	? ; Number of bytes actually read
89.		
90.	end	

Listing 7.2: Main program to display in both binary and ASCII

- Line 64: Macro disp calls subroutine v_bin1 to display a byte in binary and then outputs a tab character. If this was the only use of macro disp, it would not have been worth it. Notice that it is not obvious in the code which registers are being used (and not saved) by a macro unless it is clearly documented.
- Line 65: Macro disp calls subroutine v_asc1 to display a byte in ASCII and then output a string containing both a carriage return and line feed. This one line replaced both lines 54 and 55 from Listing 6.2 that performed the same thing.

Three source files are now present and must be compiled and linked:

1. Main program that reads input text line from the user and echoes each input character in binary and ASCII
2. File containing display subroutines v_asc and v_asc1 along with v_opn from the previous chapter
3. The new v_bin1 subroutine for displaying a byte in binary.

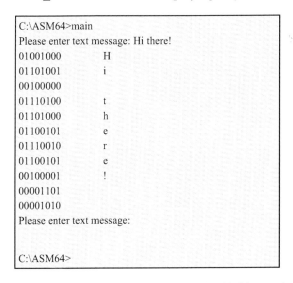

```
C:\ASM64>main
Please enter text message: Hi there!
01001000        H
01101001        i
00100000
01110100        t
01101000        h
01100101        e
01110010        r
01100101        e
00100001        !
00001101
00001010
Please enter text message:

C:\ASM64>
```

Listing 7.3: Loop of multiple input text characters echoed in binary and ASCII

As discussed in the previous chapter, several approaches are available to generate the executable main program from multiple source files. Each source file could be compiled separately, a library could be built, or everything could be compiled and linked with one command line. Since this is a very small program, I chose the latter approach, and its one line is shown below.

ML64 main.asm v_asc.asm v_bin1.asm /link /SUBSYSTEM:CONSOLE /ENTRY:main

Hexadecimal Display

What's wrong with binary? Why use hexadecimal (base 16)? The simple answer is hexadecimal is compact, and it is very easy for us humans to convert between binary and hexadecimal.

Binary numbers are awkward for us due to the large number of columns required. Who would prefer replacing the decimal representation of 7094, 1620, 1108, 6600, 3033, and 7800 with their binary equivalents 1101110110110, 11001010100, 10001010100, 1100111001000, 101111011001, and 1111001111000? Conversion between binary and decimal is difficult to do "in our heads." The difficulty stems from the fact that 10 is not an integer power of 2, but base 16 is 2^4 thereby making it easy to convert every 4-bit binary pattern to a hexadecimal digit.

Conversion from binary to hexadecimal is done from right to left as shown in Figure 7.9. If the number of binary bits is not a multiple of four, then the high order "missing" bit positions will be filled with zeroes. Please see Appendix H for more information on hexadecimal if you like.

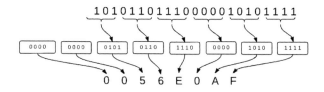

Figure 7.9: Binary reduced to hexadecimal

Subroutine v_hex1 is similar to subroutine v_bin1 except four bits are shifted and masked at one time instead of just one bit. Since there are only two hex digits in an 8-bit byte, no loop will be needed. Instead, the first digit will be obtained by a logical shift to the right, and the second is obtained with a logical AND.

- Line 10: Register RBX points to a translation table to be used with the XLAT instruction on lines 13 and 18.

- Line 12: The first 4-bit nibble is obtained by a logical shift as shown if Figure 7.10.
- Line 13: The XLAT instruction indexes into the translation table to convert the value in register AL from a 4-bit nibble to a hex digit.
- Line 17: The second 4-bit nibble is obtained with a 4-bit mask with an AND instruction as shown if Figure 7.11.
- Line 18: The XLAT instruction indexes into the translation table to convert the value in register AL from a 4-bit nibble to a hex digit.
- Lines 29 and 30: Byte array of 16 ASCII characters representing 16 hexadecimal digits

```
1. ;          Subroutine v_hex1 displays one byte in hexadecimal.
2. ;          R12: Points to the byte in memory
3. ;          Registers preserved: RBX,RBP,RDI,RSI,RSP,R12-R15
4.
5. v_asc   proto              ; Declare external subroutine.
6.         .code
7. v_hex1  proc               ; Subroutine v_bin1 entry point
8.         push   RBX         ; Save RBX and decrement RSP by 8
9.         lea    RDX,nib2     ; Points to 2-byte memory buffer
10.        lea    RBX,dig      ; Pointer to list of hex digits
11.        mov    AL,[R12]     ; Load byte to be displayed
12.        shr    AL,4         ; Right justify first nibble
13.        xlat                ; Convert 4-bit nibble to hex digit
14.        mov    [RDX],AL     ; Store high-order hex digit.
15.
16.        mov    AL,[R12]     ; Reload byte to be displayed
17.        and    AL,1111b     ; Mask off all but second nibble.
18.        xlat                ; Convert 4-bit nibble to hex digit
19.        mov    [RDX+1],AL   ; Store low-order hex digit.
20.
21.        mov    R8,2         ; Number of characters to display
22.        call   v_asc        ; Subroutine that displays ASCII
23.
24.        pop    RBX          ; Reload RBX and reposition stack
25.        ret                 ; Return to the calling program
26. v_hex1 endp
27.
28.        .data
29. dig    byte   "0123456789" ; ASCII string of digits 0 through 9
30.        byte   "ABCDEF"     ; ASCII string of digits A through F
31. nib2   byte   2 DUP (?)    ; Memory buffer for display
32.        end
```

Listing 7.4: Subroutine to output hexadecimal number in ASCII

7: Binary & Hexadecimal

95

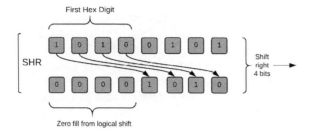

Figure 7.10: Isolate first hex digit using logical shift instruction.

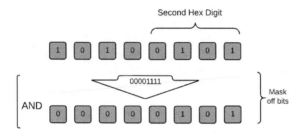

Figure 7.11: Isolate second hex digit using AND instruction.

The only modifications made to the main program as shown in Listing 7.5 is to include a hexadecimal display. The disp macro is now even more useful because it is called three times: binary, hexadecimal, and ASCII. Since the modifications are so minimal, I have only shown the changes and the inner loop which calls the three subroutines. The Listing_7_5.txt file in GitHub is complete, however.

- Line 11: Declare external subroutine v_hex1
- Line 66: Call subroutine for hexadecimal display followed by a tab.

11. v_hex1	proto		; Display byte in hexadecimal
65. inloop:	disp	v_bin1,tab	; Display byte as 8 bits.
66.	disp	v_hex1,tab	; Display byte as 2 hex digits/
67.	disp	v_asc1,newln	; Display byte as ASCII character.
68.	inc	R12	; Set pointer to next character.
69.	dec	R13	; Decrement number of bytes remaining.
70.	jg	inloop	; Continue loop until message complete.

Listing 7.5: Changes to main.asm to support hexadecimal output

LIB Example

There are now four assembly language source code files: main.asm, v_asc.asm, v_bin1.asm, and v_hex1.asm. The main executable can be generated by placing the four source code files on the ML64 command line followed by the LINK command and its options. This is fine for such a small program. However, in the spirit of building larger systems, we can also generate the executable with the following three commands.

1. ML64 /c v_asc.asm v_bin1.asm v_hex1.asm
2. LIB /out : v.lib /verbose v_asc.obj v_bin1.obj v_hex1.obj
3. ML64 main.asm /link /SUBSYSTEM : CONSOLE /ENTRY : main

The first line assembles the files containing the subroutines into three object code files. The second line builds a library named v.lib that contains all the subroutines. The third line builds the executable and finds the needed subroutines in the v.lib file. Note: The main program has a "includelib v.lib" statement, similar to the one for kernel32.lib.

Listing 7.6 shows a sample output displaying binary, hexadecimal, and ASCII for each character that was entered. Notice that the last two characters are hexadecimal 0D and 0A which represent "control characters" carriage return and line feed, respectively.

```
C:\ASM64>main
Please enter text message: Hi there!
01001000          48          H
01101001          69          i
00100000          20
01110100          74          t
01101000          68          h
01100101          65          e
01110010          72          r
01100101          65          e
00100001          21          !
00001101          0D
00001010          0A
Please enter text message:

C:\ASM64>
```

Listing 7.6: Each input byte is echoed in binary, hexadecimal, and ASCII.

Review Questions

1. Subroutine v_bin1 (Listing 7.1) supports some of the requirements of the X64 Calling Convention. What is missing? Why is it necessary that some requirements be met? Hint: See v_asc coding in Chapters 5 and 6. What is the advantage, and why is it OK that not all of the requirements be met?

2. * Even though subroutine v_asc does not fully abide by the X64 Calling Convention, why must the RSP stack pointer be 16-byte aligned by the push instruction on line 8 of subroutine v_bin in Listing 7.1?

3. What is meant by a "bitwise" logical operation?

4. * Octal was a very popular base used in assembly language for many years because it is also a compact form for expressing binary numbers. Although still available, why has hexadecimal almost universally replaced it?

Programming Exercises

1. Change line 10 of Listing 7.1 to use "MOV RDI, offset bits8" instead of the LEA instruction. Although both techniques to load an address into a register provide identical results in this example, one is slightly faster and one is more general. What are the comparative advantages of OFFSET and LEA?

2. On lines 16 and 17 of Listing 7.1, reverse the order of the shift and move instructions. Also change the logical shift to a circular shift (SHC instruction), and make it always shift by 1 bit (not the value in CL). Compile, link, and execute to verify that the v_bin1 subroutine works the same with this new coding.

3. Replace the two instructions on lines 21 and 22 with a LOOP instruction. Why will CL now have to be initialized to 8 instead of 7? Why could this not have been done before the modifications to the shift and move that were done in Exercise 2 above?

4. Fill the bits8 array in reverse order. Lines 10 and 11 of Listing 7.1 will be changed to initialize RDI to bits8+7 and set the direction flag (SDF), respectively. The shift will also have to be to the right (either logical or circular will work).

— 8 —
Decimal & More

Decimal representation of a number is really a short notation for a polynomial of powers of 10. For example: 3274 is $3 \times 10^3 + 2 \times 10^2 + 7 \times 10^1 + 4 \times 10^0$. In the preceding chapter, we displayed a number in binary using a loop of repeated division by two. Because it's faster, we used shifting to perform the division. Of course, the same loop of repeated divisions would work for decimal, and here we will actually use a divide instruction because 10 is not an integer power of 2. For example, the way we display 3274 in base 10 is the following:

1. 3274 / 10 = 327 Remainder 4
2. 327 / 10 = 32 Remainder 7
3. 32 / 10 = 3 Remainder 2
4. 3 / 10 = 0 Remainder 3

Introductions

Only one X86-64 instruction is introduced in this chapter:

- DIV: Integer divide is used in the sample program. Integer multiply is also discussed.

Multiply and Divide

When two bytes, 10000000b and 10000000b (both decimal 128, unsigned) are added within a CPU, the sum is 100000000b which doesn't fit in 8 bits, so the carry flag is set if byte registers are used. Likewise, if two copies of 01000000b (64 decimal) are added, the sum is 10000000b, which fits in a byte register, but the overflow flag is set indicating a possible error (depending whether the number is considered to be signed or unsigned). Similar carry and overflow cases appear for addition in 16-bit, 32-bit, and 64-bit registers.

In the case of multiplication, it is very easy to get a product that requires more bits than its factors. For example, when 00010000b and 00010000b (decimal 16) are multiplied within a CPU, the product is 100000000b which doesn't fit in 8 bits. Actually, most combinations of two 8-bit factors have a product requiring more than 8 bits. For this reason, X86-64 instructions that multiply two 8-bit numbers result in 16-bit products, two 32-bit numbers result in a 64-bit product, and two 64-bit numbers result in a 128-bit product.

In the Intel 8086 processor, multiplication and division were very restrictive regarding which registers were used: all included either AL or AX as one of the factors. If the contents of AL were multiplied by the contents of another 8-bit register, the product was placed into AX. But when AX was multiplied by another 16-bit register, where could the 32-bit product be placed since the largest register was only 16 bits? The lower 16 bits were stored in AX while the upper 16 bits were stored in DX. That combination of the lower bits stored into an "A" register combined with the upper bits in a "D" register has been extended up to the X86-64 architecture for 32 and 64 operations as well..

Division, being the inverse of multiplication, not only reverses the above size requirements, but has two results: a quotient and a remainder. Dividing a 128-bit number dividend results in a 64-bit quotient and a 64-bit remainder. Similar sizes are present for 64-bit, 32-bit, and 16-bit dividends. Where is this 128-bit register? The X86-64 processor combines two 64-bit registers to get 128 bits, just like the 16-bit Intel 8086 combined two 16-bit registers for its 32-bit products. In both cases, the "A" register is combined with the "D" register. The X86-64 does have a special set of 128-bit and even 256-bit registers, but these are for use with the SSE and AVX extensions as described in Chapter 11. Non-integers, i.e., floating point representation, are also handled by SSE and AVX instructions as described in Chapter 12.

Display in Any Base

Subroutine v_dig1 demonstrates the division instruction with the simplest format where the dividend is in register AX and the 8-bit divisor results in the quotient in register AL and the remainder in register AH. The divisor can be any 8-bit register, any 8-bit byte variable, or even an index register pointing to a byte (i.e., BYTE PTR [BX]). This AX division example is shown on line 18 of Listing 8.1 where the number in register AX is converted into a string of decimal digits in a loop of successive divisions by 10. Actually, subroutine v_dig1 is more general than only decimal conversion because the divisor can be any integer less than 256 (i.e., not just base 10). Programming Exercise 1 includes modifications enabling v_dig1 to display in many more bases.

Notes for the v_dec1 subroutine in Listing 8.1:

- Line 11: Register RDX initial value points to the "rightmost" character position (one's place) in the string named dbuf. This is because each digit is peeled off as a remainder during each pass through the loop.
- Line 12: Register R8 will be a saved copy pointing to the one's place and will be used to calculate the number of digits to display.
- Line 16: On each pass through the loop, register RDX will be moved one digit position to the "left."
- Line 17: Register AX will be divided on the next line, so its upper 8 bits must be set to zero.
- Line 18: Register AX will be divided by the 8-bit R11B register,

resulting in the quotient in register AL and the remainder in register AH.

- Line 19: The remainder can be any whole number less than the base, and it must be mapped to a "printable character" in the range of ASCII "0" through "9." It is this instruction that limits subroutine v_dec1 to a maximum of base 10. If a different mapping is used, such as one using an XLAT instruction, then higher bases are easily possible.

1. ;	Subroutine v_dig1 displays one byte in a selected base.		
2. ;		R11: Contains the base (2 through 10)	
3. ;		R12: Points to the byte in memory	
4. ;		Registers preserved: RBX,RBP,RDI,RSI,RSP,R12-R15	
5.			
6. v_asc	proto		; Declare external subroutine.
7.	.code		
8. v_dig1	proc		; Subroutine v_dig1 entry point
9.	push	RBX	; Save RBX and decrement RSP by 8
10.	mov	AL,[R12]	; Load byte to be displayed
11.	lea	RDX,dbuf+lengthof dbuf	; Point to buffer end.
12.	mov	R8,RDX	; R8-RDX will "count" digits.
13.			
14. ;	Calculate next digit to be displayed.		
15.			
16. modX:	dec	RDX	; The position to hold next digit
17.	mov	AH,0	; Prepare a 16-bit number in AX.
18.	div	R11B	; Get quotient in AL, remainder in AH.
19.	add	AH,'0'	; Map 0 through 9 to '0' through '9'
20.	mov	[RDX],AH	; Store in array of digits.
21.	and	AL,AL	; Test if any quotient left to process.
22.	jnz	modX	; Continue until all digits done.
23. ;			
24. ;	Display all digits of current byte from memory buffer.		
25. ;			
26.	sub	R8,RDX	; Number of characters to display
27.	call	v_asc	; Subroutine that displays ASCII
28.			
29.	pop	RBX	; Reload RBX and reposition stack
30.	ret		; Return to the calling program
31. v_dig1	endp		
32.			
33.	.data		
34. dbuf	byte	8 DUP (?)	; Memory buffer for display
35.	end		

Listing 8.1: Subroutine v_dig1 displays in any base (2 through 10)

```
dispbs    10,tab  ⟹  {  mov   R11,10
                         call  v_dig1
                         msgOut tab
```

Figure 8.1: Macro expansion example that generates 3 lines of code.

The main program will be modified to display each echoed character in binary, hexadecimal, ASCII, and now decimal. A new macro, dispbs, will also be defined to assist in the calling of new subroutine v_dig1. The following notes indicate changes made to the main program from Chapter 7:

- Line 12: Declare v_dig1 as an external procedure.
- Lines 32 through 40: Macro dispbs is defined that will call v_dig1.
- Line 78: Macro dispbs will display the byte's value in base 10. Actually, any base less than 11 can be chosen, such as 8 for octal.

1.		includelib	kernel32.lib	; Windows kernel interface.
2. GetStdHandle	proto			; Function to retrieve I/O handle
3. ReadConsoleA	proto			; Function reads from keyboard
5. Keyboard	equ	-10		; Device code for console text input
5. MaxBuf	equ	20		; Maximum input buffer size
6. ExitProcess	proto			
7. v_asc	proto			; Function writes ASCII string.
8. v_asc1	proto			; Function writes one character.
9. v_opn	proto			; Function opens display stream.
10. v_bin1	proto			; Display byte in binary
11. v_hex1	proto			; Display byte in hexadecimal
12. v_dig1	proto			; Display byte in selected base (2-10)
13.				
14. ;		Macro "msgOut msg" calls subroutine to display a string.		
15. ;			msg: Label of ASCII message for command window.	
16.				
17. msgOut	macro	msg		; One argument: msg
18.	lea	RDX,msg		; Pointer to message to display
19.	mov	R8,lengthof msg		; Number of characters to display
20.	call	v_asc		; Write text to command window.
21.	endm			
22.				
23. ;		Macro "disp sub,tail" calls a subroutine, then displays a character.		
24. ;		sub:		Subroutine to be called
25. ;		tail:		Separation character to be output
26.				
27. disp	macro	sub,tail		; Two arguments: sub and tail
28.	call	sub		; Call specified subroutine

```
29.              msgOut    tail              ; Write text to command window.
30.              endm
31.
32. ;            Macro "dispbs base,tail" calls v_dig1, then displays a string.
33. ;                      base:             Base (2 - 10) for display of number
34. ;                      tail:             Separation character to be output
35.
36. dispbs       macro     base,tail
37.              mov       R11,base          ; Load base for display.
38.              call      v_dig1            ; Display number in base [R11]
39.              msgOut    tail              ; Output separation string
40.              endm
41.
42.              .code
43.
44. ;            Main program that reads text message from user through command
45. ;            window keyin and displays it in same command window.
46. ;                      1. Lines are input until only "Enter" key pushed.
47. ;                      2. Each character will be echoed on a separate line.
48.
49. main         proc
50.
51.              sub       RSP,40            ; Reserve "shadow space" on stack.
52.
53. ;            Obtain "handles" for console Input streams
54.
55.              call      v_opn             ; Open text display stream.
56.              mov       RCX,Keyboard      ; Console standard input handle
57.              call      GetStdHandle      ; Returns handle in register RAX
58.              mov       [stdin],RAX       ; Save handle for keyboard input.
59.
60. ;            Display the prompt message.
61.
62. nxtlin:      msgOut    pmsg              ; Write text string to command box.
63.
64. ;            Read input line from user keyboard.
65.
66.              mov       RCX,stdin         ; Handle to standard input device
67.              mov       R8,MaxBuf         ; Maximum length to receive
68.              lea       RDX,keymsg        ; Memory address to receive input
69.              lea       R9,nbrd           ; Number of bytes actually read.
70.              call      ReadConsoleA      ; Read text from command box.
71.
72. ;            Echo line just input back to the user one character at a time.
73.
74.              lea       R12,keymsg        ; Memory buffer containing input
75.              mov       R13,nbrd          ; Number of characters actually read
76. inloop:      disp      v_bin1,tab        ; Display byte as 8 bits.
77.              disp      v_hex1,tab        ; Display byte as 2 hex digits/
```

```
78.                    dispbs     10,tab          ; Display byte in decimal.
79.                    disp       v_asc1,newln    ; Display byte as ASCII character.
80.                    inc        R12             ; Set pointer to next character.
81.                    dec        R13             ; Decrement byte count remaining.
82.                    jg         inloop          ; Loop until message complete.
83.
84. ;                  Go get another line, but exit if only "Enter" key was input.
85.
86.                    mov        R8,nbrd         ; Length (bytes) of input message
87.                    cmp        R8,2            ; Test if only CR and LF characters.
88.                    jg         nxtlin          ; Loop back to get another input.
89.
90.                    add        RSP,40          ; Replace "shadow space" on stack
91.                    mov        RCX,0           ; Set exit status code to zero.
92.                    call       ExitProcess     ; Return control to Windows.
93.
94. main               endp
95.
96.                    .data
97. pmsg               byte       "Please enter text message: "
98. keymsg             byte       MaxBuf DUP (?)  ; Memory buffer for keyboard input
99. newln              byte       0DH,0AH         ; Carriage return and line feed
100. tab               byte       09H             ; Horizontal tab character
101. stdin             qword      ?               ; Handle to standard input device
102. nbrd              qword      ?               ; Number of bytes actually read
103.
104.                   end
```

Listing 8.2: Main program displays a byte in binary, hexadecimal, decimal, and ASCII.

```
C:\ASM64>main
Please enter text message: Hi there!
01001000        48        72        H
01101001        69        105       i
00100000        20        32
01110100        74        116       t
01101000        68        104       h
01100101        65        101       e
01110010        72        114       r
01100101        65        101       e
00100001        21        33        !
00001101        0D        13
00001010        0A        10
Please enter text message:

C:\ASM64>
```

Listing 8.3: Program execution

Table 8.1 shows the integer divide instructions available in the X86-64 architecture. The first three are the same except for the size of the operands, which are implied by the divisor in the third column which can be either a register or a memory location. In this table, *64-bit* means any 64-bit general purpose register such as RBX or R15, any 64-bit quad word memory variable, or even an index register pointing to a quad word (i.e., QWORD PTR [BX]). Note: These three instructions always have a dividend that has the upper half in a D register and the lower half in an A register. For example, the instruction "DIV R12" divides the 128-bit value in registers RDX:RAX by the value in register R12, and places the quotient in RAX with the remainder in RDX.

The fourth case was highlighted in Listing 8.1 and is somewhat different in that the dividend is entirely in one register, the 16-bit AX register. For each of the unsigned examples of DIV, there is a signed IDIV version. For example, "DIV   DL" assumes register AX has a range of 0 through 65,535, while "IDIV   DL" assumes register AX has a range of -32,768 through +32,767. Also, the status flags are not set as they would be for addition and subtraction instructions. There can even be a hardware interrupt (program jumps to a Windows error routine) if the divisor has a value of zero.

Instruction	Dividend	Divisor	Quotient	Remainder
DIV *64-bit*	RDX:RAX	*64-bit*	RAX	RDX
DIV *32-bit*	EDX:EAX	*32-bit*	EAX	EDX
DIV *16-bit*	DX:AX	*16-bit*	AX	DX
DIV *8-bit*	AX	*8-bit*	AL	AH

Table 8.1: Samples of divide instructions

Multiplication

The X86-64 architecture offers much more flexibility with multiplication than division. Instead of the factors being restricted to only the "A" and "D" registers, the following three formats are possible (determined by the number of operands). As in division, both signed and unsigned, versions are available (MUL and IMUL). The product, [RDX] : [RAX], has the high-order 64 bits placed into RDX, and the low-order 64 bits placed into RAX.

```
1. MUL    R15    ; One operand
      [RAX] * [R15]    =>    [RDX] : [RAX]
2. MUL    R14, R15    ; Two operands
      [R14] * [R15]    =>    [RDX] : [RAX]
3. MUL    R14, R15,100    ; Three operands
      [R14] * [R15] * 100    =>    [RDX] : [RAX]
```

Review Questions

1. As an exercise, convert 3274 to base seven by successively dividing by seven until the quotient is zero (3274/7 = 467 remainder 5, ...).
2. * The overflow flag sometimes indicates an error occurred and sometimes it doesn't. Why doesn't the CPU know for sure if there is an error? Hint: See Appendix G.
3. In Chapter 7, the base two display works by successive division by 2 performed by a shift instruction. Why can't a division by 10 for decimal be performed by a shift instruction?

Programming Exercises

1. Line 19 (ADD   AH,'0') of subroutine v_dig1 maps a binary digit to its ASCII equivalent. This limits subroutine v_dig1 to a maximum base of 10. Modify v_dig1 to use a translation table as was done in subroutine v_hex1 in Chapter 7. Note: Register AL will have to be used, so a little extra coding will be needed besides the translation table and the XLAT instruction.
2. Replace the disp macro calls to subroutines v_bin1 and v_hex1 in the main program with dispbs calls with base arguments of 2 and 16, respectively.
3. Modify subroutine v_dig1 so that its output is right justified. This can actually be easier coding the the original, but be sure to initialize the dbuf buffer to blanks with each call to v_dig1.
4. Generally, a signed number is negative if its high order bit is a one (bit 7 = 1 for an 8-bit value). Modify v_dig1 to output a negative number as a minus sign followed by the negative (NEG instruction) of the original value.

— 9 —
Arrays & Strings

An array is an ordered list of adjacent storage locations in memory. The list is composed of elements of a fixed size that can be bytes, words, or even a more complicated combination of bytes and words. Tables, vectors, and matrices are other names commonly associated with arrays, and many times only differ by the number of dimensions (number of rows, number of columns, etc.).

A string has traditionally referred to a byte-array of ASCII characters such as a message to be displayed. There are several "string manipulation" instructions within the X86-64 architecture, and they are not just limited to bytes, but work with words, double words, and even quad words. "String instructions" process data sequentially from beginning to end or end to beginning, while "indexing" instructions access array elements in any "random" order.

The sample program in Chapter 9 uses a variety of string and indexing instructions to copy data from one location in memory to another. It builds upon the simple keyboard echo program from Chapter 4. This program will then be extended in chapters 10 and 11 covering SIMD (Single Instruction Multiple Data) operations.

Introductions

X86-64 instructions:

- LODSQ: Load quad word from memory into register RAX. Instructions LODSB, LODSW, and LODSD are the same instruction as LODSQ except they load AL, AX, and EAX, respectively.
- STOSQ: Store RAX into quad word in memory. STOSB, STOSW, and STOSD store registers AL, AX, and EAX, respectively.
- MOVSQ: Copy a quad word from one location in memory to another. MOVSB, MOVSW, and MOVSD copy bytes, words, and double words, respectively.
- REP: An instruction prefix that turns string instructions into "hardware" loops.

Special Registers

Some of the X86-64 general purpose registers have a special purpose from both hardware and software perspectives (see Table 3.1). String instructions are limited to the following string index registers.

- RAX: Data register used in string instructions
- RSI: Source index used in string instructions
- RDI: Destination index used in string instructions
- RCX: Counter register used in REP string instructions

The line echo program, originally appearing in Listing 4.1, has been modified in Listing 9.1 with the following enhancements:

- Lines 10 through 20: Macro "txtOut" has been added to simply display a fixed length string in memory in ASCII.
- Line 53: Echoes the keyboard input buffer "as is"
- Lines 55 through 62: Loop that copies keyboard input buffer using string load and store instructions
- Line 63: Display copy of keyboard input
- Lines 84 and 85: Reserve memory for keyboard and display buffers. Note: For this first example "byte" rather than "quadword" is more appropriate for size, but upcoming modifications will need the quad word size.

1.		includelib	kernel32.lib	; Windows kernel interface
2. GetStdHandle	proto			; Function to retrieve I/O handles
3. WriteConsoleA	proto			; Function writes command window
4. ReadConsoleA	proto			; Function reads keyboard buffer
5. Console	equ	-11		; Device code for console output.
6. Keyboard	equ	-10		; Device code for console input.
7. MaxBuf	equ	40		; Maximum input buffer size
8. ExitProcess	proto			
9.				
10. ;		Macro "txtOut msg, nchar" displays a character string.		
11. ;		msg:	Address of ASCII message	
12. ;		nchar:	Address of message length	
13.				
14. txtOut	macro	msg,nchar		; Message location and length
15.	mov	RCX,stdout		; Handle to standard output device
16.	lea	RDX,msg		; Pointer to message to display
17.	mov	R8,nchar		; Number of characters to display
18.	lea	R9,nbwr		; Number of bytes actually written.
19.	call	WriteConsoleA		; Write text string to window.
20.	endm			

```
21.
22.              .code
23.
24. ;           Main program that reads text message from user through command
25. ;           window keyin and displays it in same command window.
26. ;                          1. Multiple lines are input until only "Enter" key pushed.
27. ;                          2. Each line will be output twice: as input and a copy.
28.
29. main         proc
30.
31.              sub      RSP,40           ; Reserve "shadow space" on stack.
32.
33. ;           Obtain "handles" for console I/O streams
34.
35.              mov      RCX,Console      ; Console standard output handle
36.              call     GetStdHandle     ; Returns handle in register RAX
37.              mov      stdout,RAX       ; Save handle of console display.
38.              mov      RCX,Keyboard     ; Console standard input handle
39.              call     GetStdHandle     ; Returns handle in register RAX
40.              mov      stdin,RAX        ; Save handle for keyboard input.
41.
42. ;           Display the prompt message.
43.
44. nxtlin:      txtOut   pmsg,plen        ; Write text string to command box.
45.
46. ;           Read input line from user keyboard.
47.
48.              mov      RCX,stdin        ; Handle to standard input device
49.              mov      R8,MaxBuf        ; Maximum length to receive
50.              lea      RDX,keymsg       ; Memory address to receive input
51.              lea      R9,nbrd          ; Number of bytes actually read.
52.              call     ReadConsoleA     ; Read text from keyboard input.
53.              txtOut   keymsg,nbrd      ; Write text back to command box.
54.
55. ;           Copy message to a second buffer and display it, too.
56.
57.              lea      RSI,keymsg       ; Pointer to input buffer
58.              lea      RDI,dismsg       ; Pointer to display buffer
59.              mov      RCX,MAXBUF       ; Size of buffer in bytes
60. cpylp:       lodsb                     ; Load next byte and inc RSI.
61.              stosb                     ; Store byte from AL and inc RDI.
62.              loop     cpylp            ; Continue until all copied.
63.              txtOut   dismsg,nbrd      ; Display new copy.
64.
65. ;           Go get another line, but exit if only "Enter" key was input.
66.
67.              mov      R8,nbrd          ; Length (bytes) of input message
68.              cmp      R8,2             ; Test if only CR and LF characters.
69.              jg       nxtlin           ; Loop back to get another input.
```

9: Arrays & Strings

70.			
71.	add	RSP,40	; Replace "shadow space" on stack
72.	mov	RCX,0	; Set exit status code to zero.
73.	call	ExitProcess	; Return control to Windows.
74. main	endp		
75.			
76.	.data		
77. pmsg	byte	"Please enter text message: "	
78.	align	16	
79. plen	qword	lengthof pmsg	; Number of bytes in prompt message.
80. stdout	qword	?	; Handle to standard output device
81. nbwr	qword	?	; Number of bytes actually written
82. stdin	qword	?	; Handle to standard input device
83. nbrd	qword	?	; Number of bytes actually read
84. keymsg	qword	MaxBuf DUP (?)	; Memory buffer for keyboard input
85. dismsg	qword	MaxBuf DUP (?)	; Memory buffer for display
86.	end		

Listing 9.1: Loop that copies keyboard buffer to display buffer

Assembling, linking, and executing the main program in Listing 9.1 is as simple as that for the single source file used in chapters 3 and 4. Listing 9.2 shows a sample execution where a line of text is input from the keyboard, and the program displays it twice: once from the input buffer and once from a copy of the input buffer. The first echo of the input line verifies that the input buffer has been filled, while the second verifies that the string copy has been successful. Entering only the "Enter" key terminates the program.

```
C:\ASM64> PATH  C:\######\Hostx64\x64;%PATH%
C:\ASM64> COPY  X64_Asm-master\Listing_9_1.txt main.asm
C:\ASM64> ML64 main.asm /link /SUBSYSTEM:CONSOLE /ENTRY:main
C:\ASM64>main
Please enter text message: First test - 123
First test - 123
First test - 123
Please enter text message: Another test!
Another test!
Another test!
Please enter text message:

C:\ASM64>
```

Listing 9.2: Program execution

String instructions were first introduced in Chapter 7 in the v_bin1 subroutine. There in Listing 7.1 and Figure 7.1, instruction STOSB stored the value in the AL register into the memory location pointed to by register RDI, and then RDI was automatically incremented to the next memory location to be filled. Since the direction flag was 0, RDI was incremented, but if it was 1, then RDI would have been decremented. In that subroutine, I used the CLD instruction to make sure the flag was clear because the states of the flags in the RFLAGs register are not guaranteed in the X64 Calling Convention.

Although the direction flag register is clear when a Windows program starts, it is still a good idea to precede a copy-loop, such as that in Listing 9.1, with a CLD instruction. I could have used the STD instruction to set the direction flag if I had wanted to fill the array in reverse order (see Programming Exercise 1).

The LODSB instruction is similar to the STOSB instruction except the data pointed to by the source index register RSI is loaded into byte register AL. Register RSI is then either incremented or decremented depending on the state of the direction flag. As shown in Table 9.1, the X86-64 architecture has been expanded to include loading the EAX and RAX registers in addition to the AL and AX options available with the original 8086.

Instruction	Register loaded from [RSI]	RSI incremented or decremented by ...
LODSB	AL	1
LODSW	AX	2
LODSD	EAX	4
LODSQ	RAX	8

Table 9.1: Four variations of the LODS instruction

Listing 9.3 shows a modification to the program where each pass through the copy loop moves 16 bits at a time. Similar modifications can be made to move 32 and 64 bits at a time.

```
57.        lea     RSI,keymsg      ; Pointer to input buffer
58.        lea     RDI,dismsg      ; Pointer to display buffer
59.        mov     RCX,MAXBUF      ; Size of buffer in words
60. cpylp: lodsw                   ; Load next word and inc RSI.
61.        stosw                   ; Store word from AX and inc RDI.
62.        loop    cpylp           ; Continue until all copied.
```

Listing 9.3: Loop that copies 16 bits at a time

Little Endian

Listing 9.4 alters the same copy loop, but couples a LODSQ instruction to load the RAX register with a STOSB instruction to store only the AL register. Obviously, data will be lost in this copy as is illustrated by the program execution in Listing 9.5

```
57.          lea     RSI,keymsg      ; Pointer to input buffer
58.          lea     RDI,dismsg      ; Pointer to display buffer
59.          mov     RCX,MAXBUF      ; Size of buffer in bytes
60. cpylp:   lodsq                   ; Load next quad and inc RSI.
61.          stosb                   ; Store byte from AL and inc RDI.
62.          loop    cpylp           ; Continue until all copied.
```

Listing 9.4: Loop with LODSQ and STOSB

Are you surprised that "AIQY" is displayed from the copied buffer and not "HPX6"? In other words, did you expect register AL to contain the letter "H" being the eighth letter input instead of "A" which was the first?

```
C:\ASM64>main
Please enter text message:
ABCDEFGHIJKLMNOPQRSTUVWXYZ123456789
ABCDEFGHIJKLMNOPQRSTUVWXYZ123456789
AIQY
Please enter text message:

C:\ASM64>
```

Listing 9.5: Loop with LODSQ and STOSB

If you step through the first four passes through the loop, register RAX will contain the following values. Note: After going through Chapter 13 using the interactive debugger, come back to this program and single step through it to watch the registers change.

- First RAX contents: "HGFEDCBA"
- Second RAX: "PONMLKJI"
- Third RAX: "XWVUTSRQ"
- Fourth RAX: "654321ZY"

Does this seem to be backwards? It's what is known as "little endian" format. As seen in Figure 9.1, the first byte from the memory buffer is loaded first into the "little end" (i.e., bit 0) of the register, and the succeeding bytes keep moving in until the "big end" is reached.

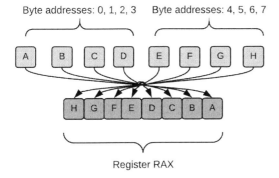

Figure 9.1: Demonstrates "Little Endian"

Figure 9.2 shows where each byte loaded into register RAX on the first three passes come from in the buffer.

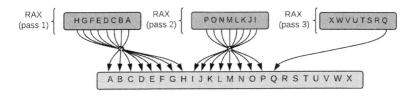

Figure 9.2: Three passes through the copy loop

Not all "byte-addressable" computers use little endian. Mainframe computers from the 1960s used big endian, while mini-computers in the 1970s typically used little endian as did microcomputers like the Intel 8086. The ARM architecture even has a processor state register bit that can switch between big and little endian formats.

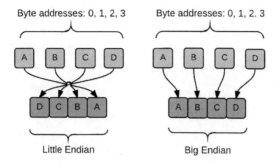

Figure 9.3: Difference between little and big endian formats

Outside of some possible memory bus hardware advantage, is there any software advantage of little endian over big endian? One advantage is automatic casting (changing types) for small constants in memory. As seen in Figure 9.4, the same pattern in memory works with byte, word, double word, and quad word values.

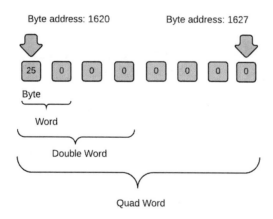

Figure 9.4: Same value if loaded into AL, AX, EAX, or RAX.

The X86-64 architecture has one memory to memory instruction: MOVS. Listing 9.6 shows a modification to the copy loop where the MOVSQ instruction copies the quad word from memory location [RSI] to memory location [RDI], and then increments both RSI and RDI. Bytes, words, and double words can also be copied using MOVSB, MOVSW, and MOVSD, respectively.

57.	lea	RSI,keymsg	; Pointer to input buffer
58.	lea	RDI,dismsg	; Pointer to display buffer
59.	mov	RCX,MAXBUF	; Size of buffer in quad words
60. cpylp:	movsq		; Copy next quad and inc RSI,RDI.
61.	loop	cpylp	; Continue until all copied.

Listing 9.6: Copy program using MOVSQ instruction

Instruction Prefixes

The above copy can actually be reduced to just one instruction. The X86 architecture has always had a repeat "prefix" that will continuously execute a single string instruction, decrement the RCX register on each pass, and continue to do so until RCX reaches zero. Not only can the REP work with the MOVS instructions as shown in Listing 9.7 to copy a text "string," but also with the STO instructions for initializing an array to some fixed value.

57.	lea	RSI,keymsg	; Pointer to input buffer
58.	lea	RDI,dismsg	; Pointer to display buffer
59.	mov	RCX,MAXBUF	; Size of buffer in quad words
60.	rep	movsq	; Copy block of memory.

Listing 9.7: Repeat prefix used with string instruction

Two other instructions that can work with the REP prefix are CMPS (Compare String) and SCAS (Scan String). These can search for a particular value in an array or string.

Indexed Addressing

Most of the common arithmetic and logical X86-64 instructions involve a register and a second operand in one of the following formats: Immediate, Register, Direct, and Scaled Index.

1. Immediate: ADD   R15, Const
   A constant is added to a register.
2. Register: ADD   R15, R14
   The contents of two register are added.
3. Direct: ADD   R15, MemLoc
   The contents of a memory location are added to the contents of a register.
4. Scaled Index: ADD   R15, [R14+8*R13+Const]
   The address of a memory location is calculated from the sum of 1) the contents of a "base" register, 2) the contents of an "index" register times a scale factor of 1, 2, 4, or 8, and 3) a constant. The contents of this calculated memory location is then added to the contents of a register.

In the above examples, Const refers to a constant known at assembly time such as the integer 137, and MemLoc refers to a label in the data area such as the name of an array. I used registers R13, R14, and R15 in the examples, but almost any of the general purpose registers will work. The examples used ADD, but MOV, SUB, and logical instructions like AND also work.

The Direct format can be thought of as a special case of the Scaled Index format, where the base and index registers are ignored. Other "special cases" of the Scaled Index format are the following:

1. Base Relative plus Index: ADD   R15, [R14+R13+Const]
   This is like the Scaled Index format where the scale factor equals 1. An alternate format is "ADD   R15, MemLoc[R14+R13]" where MemLoc is a label in the data area (such as the beginning of an array).
2. Base plus Index: ADD   R15, [R14+R13]
   The sum of the contents of registers R14 and R13 points to a memory location containing a value to be added to the contents of register R15. This is like the Scaled Index format where the scale factor equals 1 and the constant equals 0.
3. Register Relative: ADD   R15, [R14+Const]
   An alternate format is "ADD   R15, MemLoc[R14]" where MemLoc is simply a label in the data area (such as the beginning of an array).
4. Register Indirect: ADD   R15, [R14]
   The "base" register R14 points to a memory location containing a value to be added to the contents of register R15.

Listing 9.8 shows the previous copy program using the Scaled Index instruction format to copy one array to another, one quad word at a time. Of course, the power of this "indexing" format is in randomly indexing into an array rather than sequentially stepping through it.

57.		lea	R13,keymsg	; Pointer to input buffer
58.		lea	R14,dismsg	; Pointer to display buffer
59.		mov	RCX,MAXBUF	; Buffer size in quad words
60.		xor	R15,R15	; Initialize index to zero.
61.	cpylp:	mov	R12,[R13+8*R15]	; Load next quad.
62.		mov	[R14+8*R15],R12	; Store 64-bits into buffer.
63.		inc	R15	; Increment index by 1.
64.		loop	cpylp	; Continue until all copied.

Listing 9.8: Copy using Scaled Index format instructions

Listing 9.9 is basically the same as Listing 9.8, except registers R13 and R14 are no longer needed since the Scaled Index MOV instructions in the copy loop now point to the beginning of each array. Note: The option "/LARGEADDRESSAWARE:NO" will be needed for the linker. Put it at the end of the ML64 command line.

57.		mov	RCX,MAXBUF	; Buffer size in quad words
58.		xor	R15,R15	; Initialize index to zero.
59.	cpylp:	mov	R12,keymsg[8*R15]	; Load next quad.
60.		mov	dismsg[8*R15],R12	; Store 64-bits into buffer.
61.		inc	R15	; Increment index by 1.
62.		loop	cpylp	; Continue until all copied.

Listing 9.9: Copy using Scaled Index format instructions

Instead of using register R15 as an index, register RCX can be both the counter and the index, but the array will be copied from end to beginning instead of beginning to end. See Programming Exercise 3 for details.

Review Questions

1. Which combination of LODS and STOS in the in Listing 9.4 would be used to convert ASCII to Unicode?
2. * Using the Scaled Index format, what instruction would implement ARRAY[I] = 6 if register EDX contained the value 6, ARRAY is an array of 32-bit integers, and register R15 represents the index I?
3. Why do arrays in most programming languages today begin with an index of zero instead of one? Also, why do we number bits within a register beginning with zero instead of one? Appendix G may have some hints.
4. Why isn't the "little end" (i.e., the "low order" bit) of a register on the "left side"? Wouldn't that solve some of the confusion with little endian? Hint: See Appendix G.

Programming Exercises

1. Alter the string copy loop in Listing 9.1 to copy in the reverse direction (RSI and RDI being decremented). You will need the STD instruction and probably the LENGTHOF directive.
2. Modify Listing 9.4 to convert from Unicode to ASCII. The ReadConsoleA function will have to be changed to ReadConsoleW to get Unicode, and the copy loop will need LODSW with LODSB.
3. * Modify Listing 9.9 to copy the buffer from the end to the beginning by using register RCX as both the array index and loop counter. Hint: Use "R12,keymsg[8*RCX-8]" instead of "R12,keymsg[8*R15]"

— 10 —
Parallel Logic

Application developers and users always want better performance, and electronics designers have generally been able to fulfill those expectations for decades. Of course, whenever one application is satisfied, another one that was previously "impossible" whets the appetite of application developers for continued performance enhancements. "Moore's Law" implies that computer performance will double every 18 months, mostly due to improvements in the packing density of transistors on integrated circuits. Oddly enough, this has proven to be the case for over three decades, far longer than many of us thought possible.

One way to improve performance is to perform multiple operations in parallel. Chapter 10 introduces parallel operations using logical instructions that have been available on almost all computers for decades. Chapters 11 and 12 will present the SSE and AVX extensions within the X86-64 architecture that provides parallelism for arithmetic operations.

Introductions

X86-64 instructions:

- OR: Logical Inclusive OR (64 simultaneous logical operations)
- XOR: Logical Exclusive OR (64 simultaneous logical operations)

Case Conversion Example

The copy program from Chapter 9 will now be slightly modified to use logical instructions to change the case of letters entered at the keyboard. As already seen in Chapter 7, the logical instructions in almost all CPUs are "bitwise" logical operations:

- In the 64-bit X86-64 registers, sixty-four logical operations are performed independently and in parallel. Logical operations can also be performed 32, 16, and even 8 bits at a time by specifying the appropriate sized registers or memory locations.
- For example, in an "OR R12, R13" instruction, bit 0 of register R12 is ORed with bit 0 of R13, and the result is placed back into bit 0 of R12. Likewise, bit 1 of R12 is ORed with bit 1 of R13, and the result is placed into bit 1 of R12. The remaining 62 bits are similar.

In ASCII, the difference between the character code for a lower case letter and an upper case letter is bit 5. As shown in Figure 10.1, the upper case "A" can be changed to lower case by setting bit 5. This can either be done through addition or the inclusive OR, both of which are commonly represented by the plus sign.

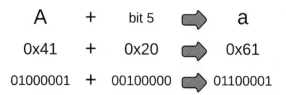

Figure 10.1: Convert upper case ASCII letter to lower case

The three logical operators available in almost every computer architecture are the AND, the inclusive OR, and the exclusive OR. Their truth tables, as well as the X86 operator names, are provided in Figure 10.2. We have already used the AND operation in previous chapters, so we will now use the XOR (exclusive OR) to switch the case of letters and the OR (inclusive OR) to force letters to lower case.

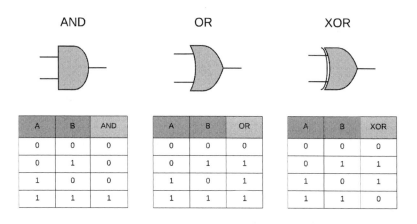

Figure 10.2: Truth tables for the logical AND, OR, and exclusive OR operations

The program in Listing 10.1 is a stand-alone program without any subroutines. It performs the following:

1. Prompts the user and reads a text line from the keyboard.
2. Echoes the input line back to the user the same as it was received.
3. Toggles the "case" of the first eight bytes, where lower case letters are converted to upper case, and upper case letters are converted to lower case. The entire text line will then be displayed. Warning: If non-alpha characters are in the first eight bytes, unusual conversions may take place.
4. Convert the first eight bytes to lower case. The entire text line will then be displayed again.
5. Continue the above four steps until a blank line is input.

1.		includelib kernel32.lib	; Windows kernel interface
2. GetStdHandle	proto		; Function to retrieve I/O handles
3. WriteConsoleA	proto		; Function writes command window
4. ReadConsoleA	proto		; Function reads keyboard buffer
5. Console	equ	-11	; Device code for console text output.
6. Keyboard	equ	-10	; Device code for console text input.
7. MaxBuf	equ	40	; Maximum input buffer size
8. ExitProcess	proto		
9.			
10. ;		Macro "txtOut msg, nchar" displays a character string.	
11. ;		msg:	Address of ASCII message
12. ;		nchar:	Address of message length
13.			
14. txtOut	macro	msg,nchar	; Message location and length
15.	mov	RCX,stdout	; Handle to standard output device
16.	lea	RDX,msg	; Pointer to message to display
17.	mov	R8,nchar	; Number of characters to display
18.	lea	R9,nbwr	; Number of bytes actually written.
19.	call	WriteConsoleA	; Write text string to window.
20.	endm		
21.			
22.	.code		
23.			
24. ;		Main program that reads text message from user through command	
25. ;		window keyin and displays it in same command window.	
26. ;		1. Multiple lines are input until only "Enter" key pushed.	
27. ;		2. Each line will be output "as is" and two case changes.	
28.			
29. main	proc		
30.			
31.	sub	RSP,40	; Reserve "shadow space" on stack.
32.			

```
33. ;                           Obtain "handles" for console I/O streams
34.
35.         mov     RCX,Console     ; Console standard output handle
36.         call    GetStdHandle    ; Returns handle in register RAX
37.         mov     stdout,RAX      ; Save handle of console display.
38.         mov     RCX,Keyboard    ; Console standard input handle
39.         call    GetStdHandle    ; Returns handle in register RAX
40.         mov     stdin,RAX       ; Save handle for keyboard input.
41.
42. ;                           Display the prompt message.
43.
44. nxtlin:    txtOut   pmsg,plen     ; Write text string to command box.
45.
46. ;                           Read input line from user keyboard.
47.
48.         mov     RCX,stdin       ; Handle to standard input device
49.         mov     R8,MaxBuf       ; Maximum length to receive
50.         lea     RDX,keymsg      ; Memory address to receive input
51.         lea     R9,nbrd         ; Number of bytes actually read.
52.         call    ReadConsoleA    ; Read text string from command box.
53.         txtOut  keymsg,nbrd     ; Write text back to command box.
54.
55. ;                           Change case of first 8 letters and echo again
56.
57.         mov     R13,keymsg      ; First 8 bytes of message.
58.         xor     R13,qword ptr [cvt]   ; "Flip" the letter case.
59.         mov     keymsg,R13      ; Overlay start of message.
60.         txtOut  keymsg,nbrd     ; Display whole message.
61.
62. ;                           Convert to lower case and echo again
63.
64.         or      R13,qword ptr [cvt]   ; Convert to lower case.
65.         mov     keymsg,R13      ; Overlay start of message.
66.         txtOut  keymsg,nbrd     ; Display whole message.
67.
68. ;                           Go get another line, but exit if only "Enter" key was input.
69.
70.         mov     R8,nbrd         ; Length (bytes) of input message
71.         cmp     R8,2            ; Test if only CR and LF characters.
72.         jg      nxtlin          ; Loop back to get another input.
73.
74.         add     RSP,40          ; Replace "shadow space" on stack
75.         mov     RCX,0           ; Set exit status code to zero.
76.         call    ExitProcess     ; Return control to Windows.
77. main    endp
78.
79.                 .data
80. pmsg    byte    "Please enter text message: "
81.         align   16              ; Set up for quad words alignment
```

82. plen	qword	lengthof pmsg	; Number of bytes in prompt message.
83. stdout	qword	?	; Handle to standard output device
84. nbwr	qword	?	; Number of bytes actually written
85. stdin	qword	?	; Handle to standard input device
86. nbrd	qword	?	; Number of bytes actually read
87. keymsg	qword	MaxBuf DUP (?)	; Memory buffer for keyboard input
88. cvt	byte	8 DUP (20h)	; Pattern to convert letter case.
89.	end		

Listing 10.1: Program that changes the case of the first eight letters input.

The following lines perform the case conversion in the above program:

- Line 58: The XOR instruction takes the exclusive OR of bit 0 from register R13 with bit 0 of first quad word in the CVT array. The same logical operation is done for the other bit positions 1 through 63. Because CVT contains eight copies of the binary pattern 00100000, the exclusive OR will toggle bit 5 of each of the eight ASCII characters loaded into R13, thereby changing their cases.
- Line 59: The result of the above 64 exclusive OR operations are stored back into the first 8 bytes of the keyboard buffer.
- Line 64: Each bit in register R13 is ORed with its corresponding bit in the CVT array, thereby changing all eight letters to lower case.
- Line 88: Eight bytes of binary 00100000 corresponding to bit 5 of each byte.

The program is compiled, linked, and executed as in the previous chapter. The following test output shows the case changes as expected. What is that "_*_*" on the last line? Please see Review Question 1 for more details.

```
C:\ASM64>main
Please enter text message: This is a test
This is a test
tHIS IS a test
this is a test
Please enter text message: AbCdEfGhIjKlMn
AbCdEfGhIjKlMn
aBcDeFgHIjKlMn
abcdefghIjKlMn
Please enter text message:
_*_*
C:\ASM64>main
```

Listing 10.2: Sample execution of changing case of first 8 letters input from keyboard

10: Parallel Logic

Review Questions

1. * In Listing 10.2, why does the program output _*_* as the last line echoed?
2. On lines 58 and 64 of Listing 10.1, why is "qword ptr [cvt]" used instead of just "cvt"?
3. Which logical instruction (AND, OR, or XOR) can clear all bits in a register to zero without using an immediate value of zero?
4. Using a logical instruction with a 64-bit register such as RAX affects all 64 bits of the register. In an instruction such as "AND EAX,0" using only the lower 32 bits, what happens in the upper 32 bits of RAX?

Programming Exercises

1. Modify Listing 10.1 to clear bit 5 of each byte which will effectively convert the first eight letters to upper case. One possible way to clear bit 5 is to AND each byte with binary 11011111.
2. Change lines 58 and 64 of Listing 10.1 to use R13D instead of R13 (dword ptr will also need to replace qword ptr). Also try R13W and R13B. Why are these three changes more examples of "little endian" format?

— 11 —
SSE & AVX

Streaming SIMD Extensions (SSE) and Advanced Vector Extensions (AVX) are two enhancements to the basic X86 instruction set to improve performance. Each consists of a set of instructions and a special register set that provide the following features not present among the original Intel 8086 instructions.

1. SIMD: Single Instruction Multiple Data (SIMD) capability where the same instruction, such as addition, is performed on multiple pairs of numbers "at the same time"
2. Floating Point: Arithmetic supporting fractions and scientific notation (very large and very small real numbers)
3. Saturation Arithmetic: Instead of setting carry and overflow flags, arithmetic operations will fill the result register with either the highest or lowest value possible for the particular data type.
4. Special Instructions: Many specialized instructions such as fused multiply/addition, square root, extreme values, etc. are now available.

From a user perspective, SSE and AVX are very similar, where SSE appeared earlier in the X86 product line with 128-bit registers. Two versions of AVX were included later, the first with 256-bit registers and AVX-512 with 512-bit registers. SSE and AVX were preceded in the X86 product line by a floating point coprocessor and MMX (multimedia extensions), both of which are now outdated.

The SSE and AVX instruction sets are very extensive, and I'm only providing a quick introduction to some of their capabilities. The program from Chapter 10 which performs logical operations in parallel will be altered in Chapter 11 to use SSE instructions and registers. A second sample program will compare saturated and non-saturated arithmetic using SIMD instructions. A floating point discussion and sample program appear in Chapter 12.

Introductions

X86-64 (SSE) instructions:

- MOVDQU: Move Unaligned Double Quad word (move a 128-bit value that does not have to be aligned on a 16-byte memory address)
- POR: Packed logical OR
- PXOR: Packed logical XOR
- PADDB: Packed addition of 8-bit integers

ML64 directives:

- XMMWORD   PTR: Pointer to 128-bit memory data type

Registers Used with SSE and AVX Instructions

The SSE and AVX instructions use their own sets of registers that are distinct from the 64-bit general purpose registers of the basic X86-64 architecture.

- XMM: 128-bit registers used with SSE instructions. Depending on the CPU version, there can be either 8 (XMM0 through XMM7), 16, or 32 XMM registers.
- YMM: 256-bit registers used with AVX instructions. Depending on the CPU version, there can be either 16 (YMM0 through YMM15) or 32 YMM registers. The lower 128 bits of each YMM register are the same as (i.e., overlap) the corresponding XMM register.
- ZMM: 512-bit registers used with AVX-512 instructions. There are 32 ZMM registers (ZMM0 through ZMM31), and the lower 256 bits of each ZMM register are the same as (i.e., overlap) the corresponding YMM register.

The program from Chapter 10 that changed the case of the first 8 ASCII characters of a text line has been modified to use SSE instructions and an XMM register. Listing 11.1 shows the modifications which now change the case of the first 16 letters of each text line (16 8-bit ASCII characters fit in each 128-bit XMM register). The program is simply assembled, linked, and executed as before giving the sample output shown in Listing 11.2.

```
55.;     Change case of first 16 letters and echo again
56.
57.      movdqu   XMM8,xmmword ptr [keymsg]   ; First 16 bytes of message.
58.      pxor     XMM8,xmmword ptr [cvt]      ; "Flip" the letter case.
59.      movdqu   xmmword ptr [keymsg],XMM8   ; Overlay start of message.
60.      txtOut   keymsg,nbrd                 ; Display whole message.
61.
62.;     Convert to lower case and echo again
63.
64.      por      XMM8,xmmword ptr [cvt]      ; Convert to lower case.
65.      movdqu   xmmword ptr [keymsg],XMM8   ; Overlay start of message.
66.      txtOut   keymsg,nbrd                 ; Display whole message.
```

Listing 11.1: Changing the case of the first 16 letters

The following lines perform the case conversion in the above program:

- Line 57: The 128-bit XMM8 register is loaded with the first 16 bytes of the keyboard buffer.
- Line 58: The SSE PXOR instruction takes the exclusive OR of bit 0 from register XMM8 with bit 0 of first double quad word in the CVT array. The same logical operation is done for the other bit positions 1 through 127. Because CVT contains sixteen copies of the binary pattern 00100000, the exclusive OR will toggle bit 5 of each of the sixteen ASCII characters loaded into XMM8, thereby changing their cases.
- Line 59: The result of the above 128 exclusive OR operations are stored back into the first 16 bytes of the keyboard buffer.
- Line 64: Each bit in register XMM8 is ORed with its corresponding bit in the CVT array, thereby changing all sixteen letters to lower case.
- Line 88: Sixteen bytes of binary 00100000 corresponding to bit 5 of each byte are in array cvt..

The program is compiled, linked, and executed as in the previous chapter. The following test output shows the case changes as expected. What is that "_*_*" on the last line? Please see Review Question 1 from Chapter 10 for more details.

```
C:\ASM64>main
Please enter text message: Hi There Everybody!
Hi There Everybody!
hI tHERE eVERYBOdy!
hi there everybody!
Please enter text message:
AbCdEfGhIjKlMnOpQrStUvWxYz
AbCdEfGhIjKlMnOpQrStUvWxYz
aBcDeFgHiJkLmNoPQrStUvWxYz
abcdefghijklmnopQrStUvWxYz
Please enter text message:
_*_*
C:\ASM64>main
```

Listing 11.2: Sample execution of changing case of first 16 letters input from keyboard

Alignment

Most computer memories, including that of the X86-64 architecture, are byte-addressable. Instructions accessing words, double words, and quad words sometimes have problems fetching the multiple bytes they need at one time. Some problems such as big and little endian amount to simply knowing the correct pattern, while other problems lead to performance degradation or hardware exception errors.

"Aligned" means that 16-bit words are loaded only from even memory addresses, 32-bit double words are loaded only from addresses that are multiples of 4, 64-bit quad words are loaded only from addresses that are multiples of 8, and 128-bit double quad words are loaded only from addresses that are multiples of 16.

Although some instructions, such as MOVDQU (Move Unaligned Double Quad word), work with unaligned data addresses, it is generally safer to organize data storage on appropriate boundaries using the "align" assembler directive.

Packed Integer Arithmetic

SSE and AVX also provide integer arithmetic operations. How do the results from an arithmetic operation such as addition or multiplication compare to one of the logical operations? Logical operations are bit-by-bit, and the results stay in each bit "column," but arithmetic operations must expand to use more bits. Even an example such as $1_2+1_2=10_2$ shows addition can have a carry that requires another bit column. In order to provide multiple simultaneous parallel arithmetic operations, the SSE and AVX instructions "pack" arithmetic operations in fixed-sized "lanes" and do not allow the results from one lane to carry into the next. For SSE instructions, the maximum number of lanes is sixteen (128-bit XMM register divided by an 8-bit lane width)

The new main program in Listing 11.3 demonstrates sixteen additions taking places simultaneously in 8-bit wide lanes. It's output shows the results of staying in each lane without carrying into the next.

1. Macro dispbs will be called to display the contents of a byte in decimal. It is identical to that already used in Chapter 6.
2. Outer loop: Add the contents of each lane to itself, and display the first eight lanes on the display screen. On each of the four iterations through the loop, the contents in each lane will double.
3. Inner loop: Although the SSE instruction adds all sixteen 8-bit lanes simultaneously, the display routine will only loop through the the the first eight values to display them.

Take note of the following lines in Listing 11.3:

- Lines 3 through 5: Subroutines from previous chapters will be called.
- Lines 7 through 17: Macro dispbs outputs one of the lanes in decimal. Note: Any base between 2 and 10 can be chosen.
- Line 35: Outer loop is initialized for four passes through the loop. More passes could be made, of course.
- Lines 47 through 51: Use SSE instructions to double the 16 8-bit integers in array intlst.

```
1.                  includelib   kernel32.lib       ; Windows kernel interface.
2. ExitProcess      proto
3. v_asc            proto                           ; Function writes ASCII string.
4. v_opn            proto                           ; Function opens display stream.
5. v_dig1           proto                           ; Display byte in selected base (2-10)
6.
7. ;                Macro "dispbs base,tail" calls v_dig1, then displays a string.
8. ;                         base:        Base (2 - 10) for display of number
9. ;                         tail:        Separation string to be output
10.
11. dispbs          macro        base,tail
12.                 mov          R11,base           ; Load base for display.
13.                 call         v_dig1             ; Display number in base [R11]
14.                 lea          RDX,tail           ; Pointer to message to display
15.                 mov          R8,lengthof tail   ; Number of characters to display
16.                 call         v_asc              ; Write text to command window.
17.                 endm
18.
19.                 .code
20.
21. ;               Main program doubles and displays contents of SSE register.
22. ;                         1. Packed addition adds multiple numbers simultaneously.
23. ;                         2. An inner loop displays each sum one at a time.
24.
25. main            proc
26.
27.                 sub          RSP,40             ; Reserve "shadow space" on stack.
28.
29. ;               Obtain "handles" for console Input streams
30.
31.                 call         v_opn              ; Open text display stream.
32.
33. ;               Make four passes through loop to double the value of each integer.
34.
35.                 mov          R14,4              ; Use R14 for loop counter.
36.
37. ;               Display first eight 8-bit integers in array intlst.
38.
39. double:         lea          R12,intlst         ; Pointer to array of 8-bit integers
40.                 mov          R13,7              ; Loop through first 7 integers
41. inloop:         dispbs       10,tab             ; Display byte in decimal.
42.                 inc          R12                ; Set pointer to next integer.
43.                 dec          R13                ; Decrement byte count remaining.
44.                 jg           inloop             ; Loop until all 7 done.
45.                 dispbs       10,newln           ; Display eighth integer.
46.
47.                 movdqu       XMM3,xmmword ptr [intlst] ; 16 8-bit integers.
48.                 paddb        XMM3,XMM3          ; Double the value in XMM3.
49. ;               paddusb      XMM3,XMM3          ; Unsigned Saturated values in XMM3
```

```
50. ;              paddsb     XMM3,XMM3    ; Signed Saturated values in XMM3
51.                movdqu     xmmword ptr [intlst],XMM3 ; Store 16 integers.
52.
53.                dec        R14          ; Decrement passes remaining.
54.                jg         double       ; Loop back to double again.
55.
56.                add        RSP,40       ; Replace "shadow space" on stack
57.                mov        RCX,0        ; Set exit status code to zero.
58.                call       ExitProcess  ; Return control to Windows.
59.
60. main           endp
61.
62.                .data
63. intlst         byte       1,2,10,50,100,150,200,250 ; Array of 8 test integers
64.                byte       8 DUP (0)    ; Fill remainder of double quad word.
65. newln          byte       0DH,0AH      ; Carriage return and line feed
66. tab            byte       09H          ; Horizontal tab character
67.                end
```

Listing 11.3: Main program adds 16 pairs of numbers simultaneously.

- Line 48: PADDB Instruction (Packed Addition, Not Saturated, Byte): This is a normal addition as would be done with the X86 ADD instruction except no carry or overflow flags are set.
- Line 49: PADDUSB Instruction (Packed Addition Unsigned Saturated Byte): Currently commented out, but will be used in the next example to limit sum to 255.
- Line 50: PADDSB Instruction (Packed Addition Signed Saturated Byte): Currently commented out, but will be used in an example to limit the sum to range of -128 to +127.
- Lines 63 and 64: List of sixteen 1-byte integers. The second eight integers are just zero, but they could have any values because we will not be looking at them in these examples.

Assemble, link, and execute the new program. The main.asm program will need external subroutines in files v_asc.asm and v_dig1.asm from previous chapters. All three source files can be compiled and linked as before. Listing 11.4 shows the execution's display.

1	2	10	50	100	150	200	250
2	4	20	100	200	44	144	244
4	8	40	200	144	88	32	232
8	16	80	144	32	176	64	208

Listing 11.4: Adding eight lanes (i.e., columns) simultaneously

The first three lanes (i.e., columns in the display) look fine, For example in lane 1: $1 + 1 = 2$, $2 + 2 = 4$, and $4 + 4 = 8$. However, in lane 4 where $50 + 50 = 100$ and $100 + 100 = 200$ is correct, a problem appears with $200 + 200 = 144$. Carry has occurred! The sum $200 + 200 = 400$, which will not fit in an 8-bit byte. The maximum unsigned value that can fit in 8 bits is 255. Similar carry problems exist for other additions shown in Listing 11.4 and summarized in Figure 11.1.

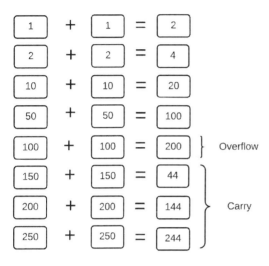

Figure 11.1 Eight lanes added in parallel with three resulting in caries and one overflow

Saturated Packed Integer Arithmetic

Is there anything that can be done about carry and overflow conditions giving ridiculous looking results? There are basically two approaches:

1. The traditional approach is simply don't use too small of a container, and avoid the problem. Depending on the application, choose a data type that is large enough to hold any possible value, whether it be word, double word, or 64-bit quad word.
2. By using "saturation" arithmetic, the X86-64 processor still won't provide the correct answer in the case of a carry, but it will keep the answer as close as possible. For unsigned bytes, the range is 0 through 255. If the result of an addition exceeds 255, then the processor will give 255 as the result. If a subtraction leads to a negative result, then the processor will give 0 as the result. For signed integer bytes, the range is -128 through 127.

There are basically twelve variations of packed integer addition and subtraction, depending on whether saturation is chosen and if the values are considered signed or unsigned. The 128 bit XMM registers can be packed as 8-bit bytes, 16-bit words, 32-bit double words, or 64-bit quad words.

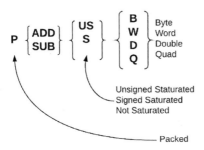

Figure 11.2: Packed addition and subtraction variations

Instruction	Sign/Saturate	Number	Range Limit
PADDB	Not Saturated	16 @ 8 bits	No limits
PADDUSB	Unsigned/Saturated	16 @ 8 bits	0 to 255
PADDSB	Signed/Saturated	16 @ 8 bits	-128 to 127
PADDW	Not Saturated	8 @ 16 bits	No limits
PADDUSW	Unsigned/Saturated	8 @ 16 bits	0 to 65,535
PADDSW	Signed/Saturated	8 @ 16 bits	-32,768 to 32,767
PADDD	Not Saturated	4 @ 32 bits	No limits
PADDUSD	Unsigned/Saturated	4 @ 32 bits	0 to 4,294,967,295
PADDSD	Signed/Saturated	4 @ 32 bits	-2,147,483,648 to 2,147,483,647
PADDQ	Not Saturated	2 @ 64 bits	No limits
PADDUSQ	Unsigned/Saturated	2 @ 64 bits	0 to 9.2×10^{18}
PADDSQ	Signed/Saturated	2 @ 64 bits	-4.6×10^{18} to 4.6×10^{18}

Table 11.1: Twelve options for SSE packed integer addition

The same program will be run two more times with a one-line alteration to demonstrate saturation arithmetic. Line 48 will be "commented out" by placing a semicolon in the first column, and either line 49 or 50 will have its comment removed. Listings 11.5 and 11.6 are the output from modifying the program using saturation addition in unsigned and signed versions, respectively.

- Line 49: PADDUSB, Unsigned Saturated, Range will be 0 to 255 for bytes.
- Line 50: PADDSB, Signed Saturated, Range will be -128 to +127.

1	2	10	50	100	150	200	250
2	4	20	100	200	255	255	255
4	8	40	200	255	255	255	255
8	16	80	255	255	255	255	255

Listing 11.5: Output Unsiged Saturated PADDUSB instead of PADDB

1	2	10	50	100	150	200	250
2	4	20	100	127	128	144	244
4	8	40	127	127	128	128	232
8	16	80	127	127	128	128	208

Listing 11.6: Output Signed Saturated PADDSB instead of PADDB

The above output of signed saturated looks a little strange with the limits being 127 and 128. The 128 is binary 10000000 which is -128 for a two's complement signed 8-bit number. Likewise, any value over 127 is really a negative number in an 8-bit signed interpretation. See Appendix G and Programming Exercise 11.1 for a further explanation.

Figure 11.3: Compare additions for 200 (-56 in signed 8-bits) and 150 (-106 if signed)

Review Questions

1. The AVX instructions are similar to the SSE instructions except they use the YMM or ZMM registers, and the instruction name begins with a "v" preceding the SSE instruction name (such as vpaddb). What would an equivalent AVX instruction for "PADDUSB XMM3,XMM3" be?
2. * The packed arithmetic instructions do not set the carry and overflow flags. How could a program rather simply check for these conditions on every lane?
3. For saturated arithmetic, there is both a signed and unsigned version (ADDUSB and ADDSB). Why is there only one version for unsaturated addition and subtraction?

Programming Exercises

1. Make a new version of the v_dec1 subroutine where it will consider bit 7 to be the sign bit. If negative (i.e., bit 7 is set), then display the minus sign followed by the negative (NEG instruction) of the byte. Rerun the saturation samples with this new v_sdec1 subroutine.
2. Make a new version of the v_dec1 subroutine where it will use 16 bit integers. Rerun the saturation samples with 16-bit PADDW instructions and this new new v_sdec2 subroutine.

— 12 —
Floating Point

Floating Point arithmetic supports the set of real numbers generally needed in science and engineering. Its internal storage format is a package similar to scientific notation, having a sign, a coefficient, and an integer exponent. Floating point hardware is not new, but has always been complicated, expensive, and relatively slow. It first appeared in computers during the 1940s, was present on most mainframes of the 1960s, and was available for the Intel 8086 using the 8087 coprocessor chip.

The SSE (Streaming SIMD Extensions) and AVX (Advanced Vector Extensions) features of the X86-64 architecture support Single Instruction Multiple Data (SIMD) floating point operations. In Chapter 12, floating point format is first discussed, and then a simple coding example is presented.

Introductions

X86-64 (SSE, AVX) instructions:

- MOVUPS: Move Unaligned Packed Single-precision value
- ADDPS: SSE addition of XMM registers containing four single precision floating point numbers
- ADDPD: SSE addition of XMM registers containing two double precision floating point numbers
- VADDPS: AVX addition of YMM registers containing eight single precision floating point numbers
- VADDPD: AVX addition of YMM registers containing four double precision floating point numbers

ML64 directives:

- REAL4: Initialize a single precision (32 bits) floating point number in memory
- REAL8: Initialize a double precision (64 bits) floating point number in memory

Floating point can be supported in software, of course, but it is extremely slow. Floating point coprocessors like the Intel 8087 and 80287 were developed as options to accompany the Intel 8086 and 80286 CPUs, respectively. Many of the complex instruction set microcomputers (CISC) that followed actually contained floating point arithmetic on the same chip.

Moving real number data (i.e., floating point) from one computer system to another was not impossible, but certainly more difficult than necessary, and it was even prone to error. The problem with the floating point formats present in the mainframes and minicomputers of the 1960s and 1970s was that although they were almost identical in concept, their implementations were incompatible. In the 1960s, even the size of a floating point number varied: 32 bits, 36 bits, 48 bits, and 60 bits were common, and double precision added another four sizes. Some computers used one's complement; some used two's complement. Most had the exponent in base 2, while one used base 16 and another base 8.

In the 1960s, ASCII was defined to address incompatibility among character sets in different computers. Likewise in 1985, the Institute of Electrical and Electronics Engineers (IEEE) standard 754 was defined to address the incompatibility among floating point formats used by various computer manufacturers. This standard was later refined in 2008, as well as becoming standard ISO/IEC/IEEE 60559:2011.

Floating Point Implements Scientific Notation

When we look at real numbers expressed in scientific notation such as 6.0221409×10^{23}, $9.10938356 \times 10^{-31}$, and $-1.60217662 \times 10^{-19}$ used in science, we observe the following:

1. The number is positive or negative
2. The significant (left of the ×10)
   - Is in base 10
   - Contains a decimal point
   - Has a precision related to the number of digits

3. The exponent (right of the ×10)
   - Can be negative or positive
   - Is in base 10
   - Is a whole number (i.e., although exponents like 5.23 are certainly allowed in mathematics, we only use integers in scientific notation)

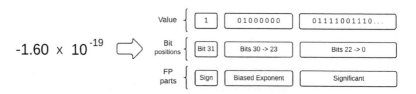

Figure 12.1: Scientific notation and 32-bit IEEE 754 floating point

So how are these base 10 real numbers with a wide range of values implemented in floating point? Figure 12.2 illustrates the floating point components and their locations within IEEE standard 754's single precision format.

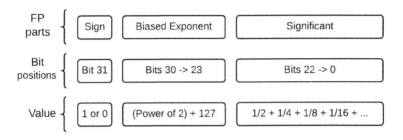

Figure 12.2: Single precision floating point fields in IEEE 754 format

Normalization

Does 220 equal 2.2×10^2 and equal 2200×10^{-1}? Of course. What about binary? Is 110_2 equal to $1.10_2 \times 2^2$ and equal to $1100_2 \times 2^{-1}$? That is also true. In scientific notation, a number is expressed in "normalized" form when it has exactly one non-zero digit to the left of the decimal point. When a floating point value is "normalized," it has exactly one non-zero digit to the left of the "binary point." This restriction leads to the following three advantages:

- Each real number is represented by a unique floating point value. Of the above three decimal choices, only 2.2×10^2 is in scientific notation. Of the above three binary numbers, only $1.10_2 \times 2^2$ is eligible for floating point format.
- Since there are only two binary symbols, and the digit left of the binary point cannot be "0," it must therefore be a "1." For this reason, the IEEE 754 format doesn't include this bit in the floating point format, and thereby "gains" an extra bit of precision.
- In "normalized" floating point format, the number of significant digits will be consistent and maximized. Note: I didn't say that the precision of all floating point numbers is equal.

The requirement of normalization was not new when it appeared in the IEEE 754 standard, but was present on all floating point hardware of the 1960s. Of course, it varied somewhat from one manufacturer's implementation to another.

Conversion to IEEE 754 Floating Point

Let's look at a couple of examples to see how a floating point number in IEEE 754 format is constructed. The first example will be the easier one to convert from base 10, since it is only a whole number and requires only the steps listed below:

1. Convert the number to base 2.
2. Normalize it.
3. Bias the base 2 exponent by adding 127, and store it into bits 23 through 30.
4. Store the fractional part of the normalized binary number into bits 0 through 22. Note: Nothing is done with the "1" that is to the left of the decimal point.

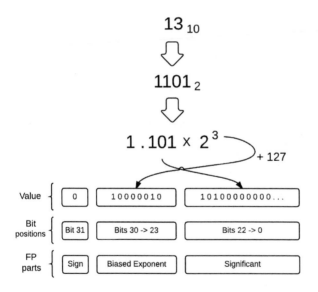

Figure 12.3: Pack 13.0 into single precision floating point fields in IEEE 754 format

Let's take a more thorough examination of the construction of floating point representation using the more complicated example shown in Figure 12.4. Although several different programing approaches can be taken, the following the steps are pretty common :

1. Set the sign bit: 1 if negative, 0 if positive.
2. Convert the base 10 exponent into a base 2 exponent

3. Convert the fraction to base 2 as the significant
4. Normalize the significant
5. Bias the base 2 exponent by adding 127, and store it into bits 23 through 30.
6. Store the significant of the normalized binary number into bits 0 through 22. Note: Nothing is done with the 1-bit that is to the left of the decimal point.

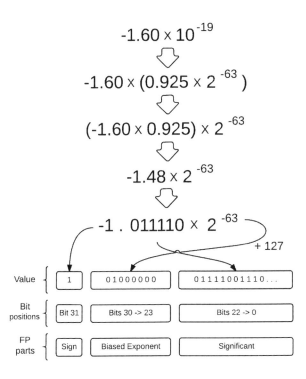

Figure 12.4: Convert scientific notation into floating point format

Why Bias the Exponent?

The obvious answer is that floating point must support a range of both positive and negative exponents. Appendix G describes four ways of indicating negative numbers: sign/magnitude, bias, one's complement, and two's complement. They all work, but why not just pick one and use it consistently? One would think that even though differences arise among different computer manufactures, at least there would be consistency within a single machine. The X86-64 uses three of the four techniques, while some computers of the past, such as the CDC 6600, have employed all four techniques for representing negative numbers.

Both one's and two's complement use the same arithmetic unit for signed and unsigned numbers. They can also extend to virtually any size "word" by combining multiple bytes using the carry flag. The bias format, on the other hand, used in the exponent, enables the integer compare instruction (CMP) to work on floating point numbers. One way to look at it is that floating point is a package, and integer format is homogeneous.

Where Did the Most Significant "1" Bit Go?

We put the sign bit into bit position 31. We biased and put the base 2 exponent into bits 23 through 30. We put the fractional part of the normalized binary number into bits 0 through 22, but we discarded what seems to be the most significant bit of all. Every additional bit included in a binary number doubles its range, so if a bit is "always" going to be the same in the floating point format, why not allow that bit position in the 32-bit word to either extend the range of the exponent or the precision of the significant? Secondly, if the bit is not there in the format, it is nearly impossible to make a non-normalized floating point number.

A Note on Normalization

I have to admit that I took a bit of liberty in the above floating point description. I did so because that description has been the one that my students have found the easiest and quickest to accept. You may find other descriptions where the bias is 128 (hex 80) because that is one half of the 256 range provided in the 8-bit exponent field. The exponent is then decremented because normalization from a hardware viewpoint has the significant being less than one.

Traditionally, a normalized floating point number is defined as one where the significant is shifted until its high order bit is a 1 bit (i.e., the significant is greater than or equal to ½, but less than 1). Unlike IEEE 754, most floating point formats did not remove the high order bit even though it "always" had to be a 1. It was even possible to generate non-normalized floating point numbers, but their use in arithmetic usually produced undesirable results. A special non-normalized case is present in the IEEE 754 standard to represent various special cases such as zero.

Not a Number (NaN)

The IEEE 754 format includes a "value" known as NaN (Not a Number) which results from operations like square root of a negative number or division by zero. There are other special cases where the exponent is either all one bits or all zero bits as shown in Figure 12.5. These cases can be generated by floating point instructions, and can also be used as operands in floating point instructions.

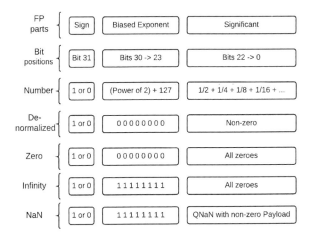

Figure 12.5: IEEE 754 floating point numbers and special cases.

The following observations can be made from Figure 12.5:

- It would be impossible to make a number that is not normalized if it were not for these de-normalized special cases. How could you normalize a floating point value of zero? You can't. That "assumed" high order 1-bit in the significant of the IEEE 754 would always get in the way. How small can a normalized number be? How small can it be if de-normalized, yet still not zero?
- All four of the special cases can be both positive and negative. Positive and negative infinity are certainly different, but positive and negative zero really are the same "value."
- Infinity is certainly "not a number" from a math perspective, but there are also other cases within the IEEE 754 standard as described below.

For an exponent of all one-bits, infinity is identified by its all-zero significant, while the two types of NaN are identified by a non-zero "Payload" (definition varies for bits 0 through 21) plus the QNaN quiet flag in bit 22:

- Signaling QNaN=0: If signaling NaN values are in one of the operands of a floating point operation, a CPU floating point interrupt will occur that requires immediate special handling by the operating system and application program.
- Quiet QNaN=1: These quiet NaN values will run through the floating point processor as smoothly as any normalized floating point number. The result will probably be another quiet NaN that will have to be examined later, but no immediate action is necessary.

Significant or Mantissa?

The terms "significant" and "mantissa" refer to the fractional part in the floating point format and are used somewhat interchangeably in the literature. The term "mantissa" has been used to describe floating point format for several decades beginning in the mid 1940s. The term "significant" is preferred in the IEEE 754 documentation apparently because "mantissa" has been associated with logarithms for centuries, and the "fraction" in the floating point format really isn't a logarithm.

Floating Point Sample Code

The function in Listing 12.1 demonstrates a couple of SSE floating point instructions in a function that simply adds 3.1416 to the input argument value. In the X64 Calling Convention, floating point augment "values" will be in registers XMM0 through XMM3 instead of integer values in registers RCX, RDX, R8, and R9, respectively.

```
1. ;        Function addPi adds Pi to a floating point value.
2. ;              XMM0: 32 bit single precision (first argument).
3.
4.           .code
5. addPi     proc
6.           movups    XMM1,pi        ; Load floating point Pi value.
7.           addps     XMM0,XMM1      ; Add Pi to argument.
8.           ret                      ; Return to the calling program
9. addPi     endp
10.
11.          .data
12. pi       real4     3.1416         ; Approximate value of Pi
13.          end
```

Listing 12.1: Subroutine showing SSE floating point instructions

- Line 2: Register XMM0 contains the value of the first floating point parameter. If the first parameter was an integer, then its value would be in register RCX, instead. XMM0 will also be used to return the floating point value of the function.
- Line 6: Move Packed Single-precision (floating point) value from unaligned address in memory to XMM1 register. Note: Registers XMM0 through XMM5 are volatile according to the X64 Calling Convention, so XMM1 can be used as scratch.
- Line 7: Floating point addition of four single precision (32 bit) numbers packed in XMM1 to the four numbers packed in XMM0.

Floating point numbers can easily be displayed from a C program, so for those interested in seeing function addPi in action, I recommend using the following C main program along with the techniques presented in the next chapter.

```
1.      #include "stdafx.h"
2.      extern "C" float addPi(float);
3.
4.      int main( ) {
5.          printf ("%1f", addPi(2.0f));
6.          return 0;
7.      }
```

Listing 12.2: Sample C main program to test addPi function

Single precision floating point functions return their values in the low-order 32-bits of the 128-bit XMM0 register. This is also the lower 32-bits of the 256-bit YMM0 register used with AVX instructions. The following AVX floating point addition can be used instead line 7 in Listing 12.1. Notice that there are three parameters: the result (YMM0) and the two numbers to be summed contained in YMM0 and YMM1. AVX instructions can put the result into a different register from the two source operands.

- VADDPS   YMM0,YMM0,YMM1

Scalars and Vectors

A scalar value consists of a single number, and a vector value consists of a group of numbers. Examples of vectors are the position and velocity of an object in a three-dimensional coordinate system which would have X, Y, and Z components, for example. An example of a scalar is the mass of an object (i.e., one number).

Why all the bother? Are vectors used that extensively that it's worth adding confusion to push for a performance gain? Consider the following:

1. In physics and engineering, quantities like position, velocity, and acceleration are all vectors that are measurable quantities.
2. Many scientific and engineering problems are solved using matrix transformations and inversions which require many vector-type multiplications and additions.
3. Graphics applications which display the 3-D world mapped onto a 2-D screen require many matrix multiplications which are efficiently processed by vector instructions.
4. Digital signal processing and many analog to digital conversions work efficiently with extensive vector processing.

Review Questions

1. * "By hand, without a computer," convert the following real numbers into single precision IEEE 754 floating point and provide the answers in hexadecimal.
   a. 128.0
   b. 9.25
   c. -9.25
   d. 0.03125
   e. 128.03125
   f. 0.0
   g. -0.0

2. * "By hand, without a computer," convert the following IEEE 754 floating point numbers from hexadecimal back into real numbers in base 10.
   a. 42a80000
   b. C1A80000
   c. 424C8000
   d. BF100000
   e. 3DCCCCCD

3. Which of the four ways to represent negative numbers described in Appendix G allows for both a positive and a negative zero?

4. In IEEE 754 floating point format, zero is represented by both the significant and the exponent being zero. If this was not the case, what value, expressed as a power of 2, would a word of all zero bits represent?

5. Why is it impossible to have a non-normalized IEEE 754 format "value"?

6. * By examining Figure 12.1, what is the smallest absolute value non-zero normalized number?

7. By examining Figure 12.1, what is the smallest absolute value non-zero de-normalized number?

8. What type of data processing would work best with quiet NaN values?

9. What type of data processing would work best with signaling NaN values?

10. * Is getting that extra 1-bit of precision in the significant more important to the single precision, double precision, or half precision format numbers?

11. * Why will multiplying by 0.1 always result in a loss of precision in binary computers?

— 13 —
IDE & C++

Some think I saved the best for the last: the Visual Studio 17 Integrated Development Environment (IDE) and applications composed of both C and assembly language. In Chapter 13, Visual Studio will be configured to properly combine C with assembly language in 64-bit mode, as well as demonstrate a program composed only of assembly language. The X64 Calling Convention and visual debugging will be included. Actually, almost all of the embedded systems that I have programmed over the years "in the real world" consist of a combination of assembly language with a higher level language like C.

Introductions

Most of the new coding is in C, but there are a couple of X86 instructions not previously appearing in an example:

- XCHG: Exchange the contents of two registers.
- LOOP: The LOOP instruction decrements RCX and jumps if RCX becomes zero. This instruction was described in Chapter 4, but individual instructions to decrement and jump were used at that time.

Calling Functions from C++

My objective of this chapter is to introduce two powerful program development techniques: Mixing assembly language with a higher level language and interactive visual debugging. As pointed out in Chapter 4, there are basically two techniques used to pass a variable's data in arguments to a function or subroutine:

- Pass by value: The value of a variable is passed in a register or on the stack, and the function has no access to the source variable itself.
- Pass by reference: The memory address of a variable is passed, and the function can actually update the variable in the calling routine's data area.

Listing 13.1 contains a very short C main program that calls two assembly language routines that calculate the sum of an array of 32-bit integers:

- fcnsum: Function that returns the sum as the return value

- thesum: Void function (i.e., subroutine) that returns the sum to a reference argument

Since this is not a book on C programming, I mostly provide details of the main program shown in Listing 13.1 that are related to calling assembly language functions:

- Line 1: This include statement is standard with Visual Studio and contains characteristics of many library functions.
- Line 2: This prototype describes the "fcnsum" function that has two arguments: 1) an array of 32-bit integers, 2) a 32-bit integer. Note: This function will return its value as a 32-bit integer. This line begins with "extern "C"" which tells the C compiler to call the function by its actual name of "fcnsum" rather than a special name that contains additional information related to object oriented programming.
- Line 3: This prototype describes the "thesum" function that has three arguments: 1) the address of a 32-bit integer, 2) an array of 32-bit integers, 3) a 32-bit integer. Note: The function will not return a function value (void), and it also begins with the special "extern "C"."
- Line 7: The void function is called, and the sum is returned to variable totalA.
- Line 8: The integer function is called, and the returned function value is stored into variable totalB in the main program.
- Line 9,10: The two sums will be printed (both will be 126).
- Line 11: Return 0 in a main program is the same as calling the ExitProcess Windows function in assembly language.

```
1.      #include "stdafx.h"
2.      extern "C" int fcnsum(int[ ], int);
3.      extern "C" void thesum(int*,int[ ], int);
4.
5.      int main( ) {
6.          int count = 3, totalA, totalB, tstdat[ ] = {11, 45, 70};
7.          thesum (&totalA, tstdat, 3);
8.          totalB = fcnsum (tstdat, count);
9.          printf ("Sum from subroutine = %d\n", totalA);
10.         printf ("Sum from function = %d\n", totalB);
11.         return 0;
12.     }
```

Listing 13.1: Main C program calling a function and a "void" function

Generally speaking, the difference between a function and a subroutine is a function returns a value and a subroutine does not. However, as seen in this example, a subroutine can return one or more values through arguments "passed by reference." In situations where only one value is returned, it is advisable to only use a function to return a value because 1) it hides the location of the actual data, 2) it is more efficient, and 3) it is expected to be done (self documenting).

- Arrays are passed by reference.
- Constants and single variables are passed by value.
- A single variable can be passed by reference if preceded by an ampersand.

Listing 13.2 provides file "sum.asm" that contains both the function and subroutine (void function) called by the C main program. Notice that the arguments appear very similar to what we have been using in all the chapters. The following lines highlight subroutine "thesum":

- Line 9: The running total is initialized with the first 32-bit integer in the array.
- Line 10: Register R8 contains the index number of the last integer in the array.
- Line 11: If the array size was only one (or less), then no more values will be added.
- Lines 12 through 14: Loop to add each of the remaining integers in the array. Note: The loop goes from the end to the beginning of the array, and each integer is composed of four bytes.
- Line 15: The 32-bit sum in register EAX is stored into the memory location pointed to by the first argument.

```
1. ;           Subroutine thesum adds a variable number of integers.
2. ;                   RCX: Memory address of variable to receive the sum.
3. ;                   RDX: Memory address of array of integer values
4. ;                   R8: Number of integers in the array
5. ;                   Supports X64 Calling Convention
6.
7.             .code
8. thesum      proc                    ; Subroutine thesum entry point
9.             mov     EAX,[RDX]       ; Load first value.
10.            dec     R8              ; Decrement number of integers.
11.            jle     retsub          ; Return with just one value.
12. thelp:     add     EAX,[RDX+4*R8]  ; Add next integer.
13.            dec     R8              ; Number of integers still to add.
14.            jnz     thelp           ; Continue with next integer.
15. retsub:    mov     [RCX],EAX       ; Return sum to calling program.
16.            ret                     ; Return to calling program
17. thesum     endp
18.
19. ;           Function fcnsum adds a variable number of integers.
20. ;                   RCX: Memory address of array of integer values
21. ;                   RDX: Number of integers in the array
22. ;                   RAX: Return calculated sum to calling program.
```

```
23. ;                        Supports X64 Calling Convention
24.
25. fcnsum    proc              ; Function fcnsum entry point
26.           xchg   RCX,RDX    ; Load RCX count, RDX with address
27.           mov    EAX,[RDX]  ; Load first value.
28.           dec    RCX        ; Decrement number of integers.
29.           jle    retfcn     ; Return with just one value.
30. fcnlp:    add    EAX,[RDX+4*RCX] ; Add next integer.
31.           loop   fcnlp      ; Continue with next integer
32. retfcn:   ret               ; Return to calling program
33. fcnsum    endp
34.           end
```

Listing 13.2: Assembly language functions called by C main program

The following lines highlight function "fcnsum" in the above listing:

- Line 26: The contents of the first two arguments are switched because the RCX register is needed for the LOOP instruction on line 31.
- Line 27: The running total is initialized with the first 32-bit integer in the array.
- Line 28: Register RCX contains the index number of the last integer in the array.
- Line 29: If the array size was only one (or less), then no more values will be added.
- Lines 30 and 31: Loop to add each of the remaining integers in the array. Note: The loop goes from the end to the beginning of the array, and each integer is composed of four bytes.
- Line 32: The 32-bit sum is already in register RAX.

Arguments	Pass by __	Location
thesum (&totalA, tstdat, 3); // a subroutine		
&totalA	Reference	[RCX]
tstdat	Reference	[RDX]
3	Value	R8
totalB = fcnsum (tstdat, count); // a function		
tstdat	Reference	[RCX]
count	Value	RDX
totalB	Value	RAX

Table 13.1: Subroutine and function arguments in example program

The C++ compiler is a console program and can be used in command mode as we have been doing with the assembler programs up to this point. It is now, however, time to move forward with the visual editor with its great debugger and file organization appropriate for developing larger programs.

Configure Visual Studio for 64-bit and Assembly Language

Visual Studio currently does not default to the 64-bit Calling Convention, nor does it default to accepting assembly language source code. Both of these options will be chosen in the following example using the source code described above in Listings 13.1 and 13.2. The following steps will be performed:

1. Create a Console Application named DemoMasm.
2. Configure Visual Studio to invoke the ML64 assembler for source files having an ".ASM" extension.
3. Put Visual Studio into 64-bit mode rather than its 32-bit default.
4. Run the DemoMasm program in debug mode showing register and memory contents in various formats.

We begin as though we are creating a normal C++ application. After starting Visual Studio, we are given the choice of creating either a Console Application or a Windows Desktop Application. Of course, assembly language can work with a Windows Desktop Application, but the user interface is more involved (pixels, locations, colors, mouse clicks, etc.) As seen in Figure 13.1, the Console Application is selected, and a solution name must be entered before clicking OK. I chose the name "DemoMasm" for the example in this book.

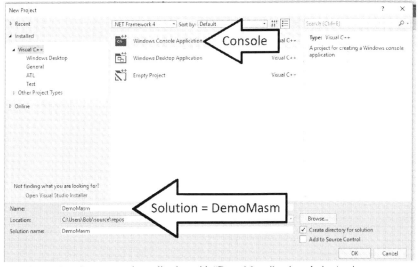

Figure 13.1: Create console application with "DemoMasm" as its solution/project name.

Visual Studio then generates a skeleton of a C++ main program. As shown in Figure 13.2, the skeleton is completely replaced by copying and pasting the code from Listing 13.1.

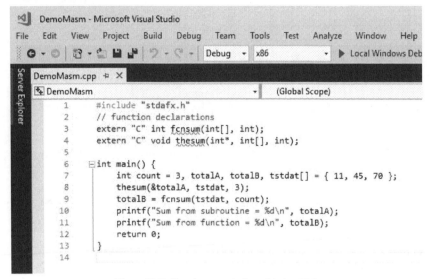

Figure 13.2: Copy/paste code from Listing 13.1.

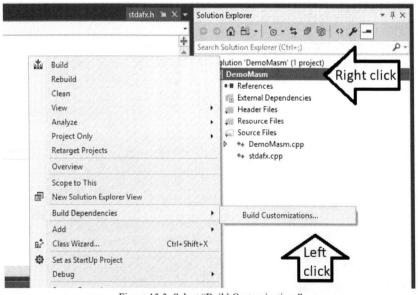

Figure 13.3: Select "Build Customizations"

Before we add a new source file containing the assembler functions, we must "Build Customizations" that tell Visual Studio what to do with files having an

".ASM" extension. First, right-click on the DemoMasm project name in the solution explorer on the upper right corner of the screen as shown in Figure 13.3. Go down to "Build Dependencies" and then over to click on "Build Customizations." Click to select the box labeled "masm (, targets, .props)" as shown in Figure 13.4, and then click OK.

Note: This .ASM assignment is in effect for all new files added to the current project and solution. This customization will have to be done on any new solutions that need assembly language.

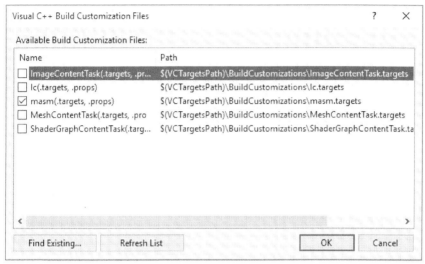

Figure 13.4: Set check box for Masm.

New source files can now be added to the project by right-clicking on the "Source Files" line in the Solution Explorer as shown in Figure 13.5. A new file can be created or an existing file can be chosen.

- New Item: Creates an empty source code file that can be keyed in (or copy and pasted). Whether Visual Studio compiles it as C++ or assembler code depends on the three character file name extension (.CPP or .ASM) provided when naming the new file.
- Existing Item: Either a C++ file with a .CPP extension or assembly language file with a .ASM extension can be chosen using the "Browse" button.

In this current example, I will "Add" a "New Item..." as shown in Figure 13.5 that then brings up the screen shown in Figure 13.6. In the next section on building a 100% assembly language program, I will take the other approach and add an "Existing Item..."

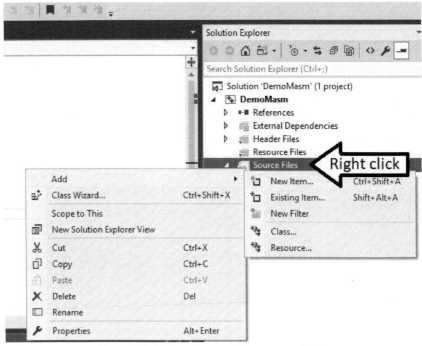

Figure 13.5: Select a new assembler source code file.

Here, select the "C++ File" even though we are adding a new assembler source code file. The file name to be created is "sum.asm" as is noted on the bottom of Figure 13.6. Then click the "Add" button to create the new empty assembler file.

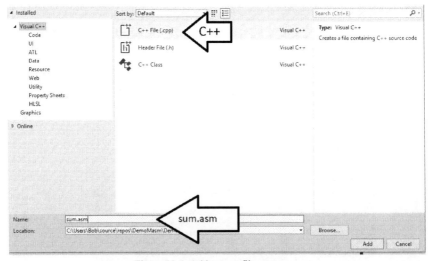

Figure 13.6: Add source file sum.asm.

The assembler source code from Listing 13.2 can now be copied and pasted into the empty sum.asm file. There is only one more configuration parameter to check: 32-bit or 64-bit mode. As shown in Figure 13.7, click on "Build" which brings down a list, and then click "Configuration Manager ..." on the bottom which brings up the "Configuration Manager" window. Here, select "X64" as the platform, and then click the Close button.

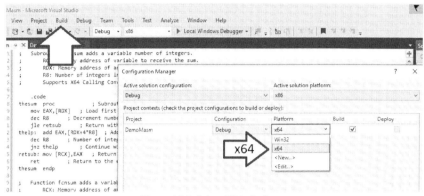

Figure 13.7: Select X64 platform.

We are now at a point where we can build the final program and even run it in debug mode. Figure 13.8 shows a break point being set by clicking in the column just left of line 12 in the assembler file. The program is then started in debug mode by pulling down the "Debug" menu and choosing "Start Debugging."

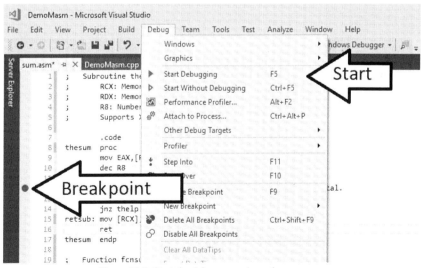

Figure 13.8: Start the debugger and run the program.

If no breakpoints are set, the program will compile, link, execute within a command window, and exit without any user interaction. If a breakpoint is set, the following screen appears. The command window will also be available, and it will usually be minimized as an entry on the task bar.

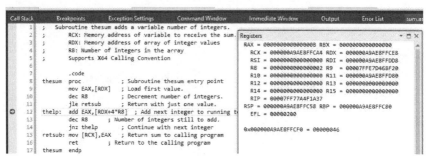

Figure 13.9: Program stopped at break point.

Interactive Debugging

The interactive debugger is usually entered when a breakpoint is reached. The following debugging features are very handy for program development and maintenance:

1. Breakpoints: By left clicking on the left side of a C or assembly language statement, a breakpoint can be set that will stop execution when the RIP register reaches that point in the program. A red dot appears when and where a breakpoint has been set. While stopped, current register and memory contents can be examined and even changed. Left clicking on an existing breakpoint's red dot will remove it.

2. Single Stepping: From a breakpoint, program execution can continue at full speed or be done one machine code instruction at a time. Register and memory contents can be examined at each step.

3. Register Contents: Not only can the general purpose registers be examined, but MMX, YMM, and ZMM registers used with SSE and AVX instructions can be also displayed.

4. Watch Windows: Four "Watch Windows" are available that show the current contents of variables in memory. One very easy way to add a variable to a watch window is to right click on it in its source code window (while stopped for a breakpoint) and then select "Add Watch."

5. Four separate blocks of memory can be examined: While stopped at a breakpoint, select pull-down list Debug, then Windows, and then Memory. An absolute address can be specified (or a label name preceded with an ampersand).

All Assembly Language

A 100% assembly language program can be built using the IDE. A second main program, in assembly language, would either be added or copied, and the default skeleton generated by the IDE in C++ must then be deleted from the project.

1. Create a new solution/project as was shown in Figures 13.1, 13.3, 13.4, 13.6 and 13.7. Note: In this new example, I give the solution the name "DemoAsmOnly" which creates a skeleton C++ main program named "DemoAsmOnly.cpp."
2. Next, I add an assembly language main program, file HelloWorld.asm from the download directory from GitHub. See screen previously shown in Figure 13.5, and use "add" followed by selecting "Existing Item," and then find the HelloWorld.asm file. Note: The program name (proc directive on lines 8 and 30 in the HellowWorld.asm assembly code) is "mainCRTStartup" which is the default name expected by the linker.
3. As shown in Figure 13.10, I then delete the skeleton C++ file by right clicking on it and then selecting Delete.

Figure 13.10: Delete C++ "skeleton" main program.

The program can now be run as before as shown in Figure 13.8. A breakpoint should be set at line 26 to keep it from immediately exiting after displaying "Hello World" in the command prompt window.

The above example has all the code in one assembly language source file. However, a program consisting of several source code files can easily be built by adding multiple .ASM files.

Review Questions

1. Name two characteristics of using "pass by value."
2. Name two advantages of using "pass by reference."
3. What is a principal danger in using "pass by reference"?
4. What are the debug function keys for "start debugging" and single stepping? How do the two single stepping commands differ from each other?

Programming Exercises

1. Rewrite the example programs to use floating point. Note: Registers XMM0, XMM1, XMM2, and XMM3 are used for the first four function arguments in floating point format if they are called by value, but since this example is not receiving floating point values in arguments, it doesn't really matter.
2. Recreate the program from Listing 8.3 which displays each input character in binary, hexadecimal, decimal, and ASCII. Lines 49 and 94 of the main program in Listing 8.2 should contain the external name "mainCRTStartup" instead of "main." Subroutines appearing in Listings 6.1, 7.1, 7.4, and 8.1 should be added (or created) as separate .ASM files.
3. Modify data in memory and registers while stopped in a debug breakpoint. For registers, just key new values on top of their current values. For variables in a watch window, first right click the particular variable in the watch window, and then choose "Edit value."

Conclusion

Aristotle is credited with the saying, "The more you know, the more you know you don't know." I look at learning assembly language not so much as a target, but as a springboard. The goal of this book is to get students and computer enthusiasts programming as quickly as possible to build a foundation for digging deeper into contemporary hardware and software architectures.

First, I recommend readers make two passes through this book: once using the command line approach and once using the IDE with its interactive debugger. This book is intended to be a "quick start" to get your "feet wet," and I now recommend readers consider going deeper into the following subjects.

Machine Code Format: Compared to most CPU machine code architectures, the X86-64 is very intricate. I recommend starting with the Intel 8086 16-bit processor architecture and migrating upward.

Technical Reference Manual: The focus of this book is to get students programming and understanding the architecture as quickly as possible using the most common instructions. You should now be at a comfortable point to understand many of the details covered in the Intel and AMD technical specification documents.

Command Line Processing: With today's graphical user interfaces, most computer users have no idea how much command line processing is being done behind the scenes. Well-rounded programmers should be comfortable developing console programs and writing command line scripts.

SSE and AVX: This book barely touches the subject of the Streaming SIMD Extensions (SSE) and Advanced Vector Extensions (AVX). SSE and AVX are whole, very elaborate, instruction sets in themselves. I wanted to limit the introduction in this book so that readers can get comfortable with a few examples before being overwhelmed by the versatility.

Interrupt Processing: In a real-time embedded systems program, there are basically two approaches that can be used to determine when a device requires attention from the software: polling and interrupts. In the polling approach, the software must loop though all possible devices, reading the status of each and deciding what to do with any status changes. This approach is very controlled and relatively easy to implement. The problem is it wastes a lot of time checking devices that do not need attention while devices that do need immediate attention have to wait their turn.

In the interrupt approach, the I/O hardware essentially "calls" a device driver (similar to a subroutine) using an "instruction" that behaves almost identical to the CALL instruction we've been using.

Supervisor Mode: The X86-64 processor design enables multiprogramming where multiple users can be sharing the same CPU and memory at virtually the same time. One responsibility of an operating system, such as Windows, is to protect one user from another while they are in the same memory space and taking turns using the CPU. This capability requires the operating system to run in a privileged, or supervisory, state where it can have access to all of memory, while user programs are restricted to their own data areas.

Windows Function Calls: In this book, I use only enough Windows API function calls to demonstrate the programming techniques and examples. File I/O, as well as task and thread management, are an important part of Windows applications development. The file I/O using "handles" is not much more complicated than the console read and write commands.

Other CPUs: The ARM processor is another very popular contemporary CPU architecture. Well-rounded computer professionals should be familiar with at least the ARM and X86-64.

Other Operating Systems: Although Microsoft® Windows® is a very popular operating system, well-rounded programmers should also have experience with other systems such as Linux, and I don't mean just at the user level, but the system calls as well.

Appendix A
Microsoft® Visual Studio®

All programming examples use the ML64.exe assembler included with the free Community Edition of Microsoft® Visual Studio 17, that is used to develop C and C++ programs running in full 64-bit mode. Many readers of this book will already have Visual Studio 17 installed on their X86-64 computers. For those of you who do not, I've included a few pointers in this brief appendix. This appendix also includes download instruction for obtaining the source code for the assembly language programs developed in this book.

Download Visual Studio 17

With Microsoft® Visual Studio 17, assembly language programs can be built using either its Integrated Development Environment (IDE) or using the ML64 assembler directly in a traditional command line approach. Both techniques are presented in this book, and each has its own merits for gaining a deeper understanding of computer software and hardware. The download is very easy from the Microsoft web site:

1. Visual Studio Community Edition is a "Free, fully-featured IDE for students, open-source and individual developers." Find the Microsoft download site by entering "visual studio 2017 community" in your favorite Internet search engine. Make sure you are downloading directly from Microsoft.
2. Visual Studio is a large application. In order to program in assembly language, only the C++ component is needed. Note: The C# compiler is different and does not need the ML64 assembler.

Source Code Download

This book contains over 30 program listings as examples of X86-64 coding. I have made them available on the Internet so they can be easily downloaded using the GitHub website. GitHub "is a code hosting platform for version control and collaboration." It is composed of multiple public and private "repositories" holding text, image, and video files. Enter the following command in your Internet browser to initiate the load of all the program listings in this book.

https://github.com/robertdunne/X64_Asm

I recommend you download and unpack the source code files into the C:\ASM\X64_Asm-master directory which I will be using in examples in the remainder of this book. If you are already familiar with and have experience with GitHub, then use a procedure with which you are most comfortable. Otherwise, please perform the following steps at the GitHub site:

1. Click on the button labeled "Clone or download" which will bring up a drop-down menu.
2. Select "Download Zip" from the drop-down menu which will download one file to your normal downloads directory.
3. You may now exit GitHub or close your browser since you will no longer need it.

From your downloads directory, perform the following to extract all the source code into C:\ASM\X64_Asm-master:

1. Right click on the X64_Asm-master.zip file just downloaded.
2. Select "Extract All..." from the pull-down menu.
3. In the "Select Destination and Extract" screen, change the file name to "C:\Asm64" or the different directory you chose for your work files.
4. Click on the "Extract" button.

The above procedure will generate most of the listing files as TXT files having file names corresponding to the captions under each listing in this book. Most will have to be copied to "main.asm" or another file name as needed. For example, the following command prompt generates the main.asm file used in the first demonstration in Chapter 2:

copy   X64_Asm-master\Listing_2_1.txt   main.asm

A few of the files will have .ASM file name extensions and will be used in Chapter 13. In addition, all GitHub repositories should have a README.md file containing pertinent information regarding the rest of the files.

Warning: The assembler source code that appears in this book and is available for download is for learning to program in assembly language. Some of these programs are incomplete and even contain problems that are used as examples. No guarantee of their commercial utility is expressed or implied.

Appendix B
Windows Command Processor

There are basically two types of user interfaces available for Windows user applications:

- Windows Console Application: Communicates with user only through text messages: Keyboard input and lines displayed in CMD window. This type of interface dates back to punch card input and line printer output in the mainframe days.
- Windows Desktop Application: Communicates with user through keyboard, mouse, and graphic images.

The Microsoft ML64 assembler is a "console" application, and so is the "visual" C++ compiler for that matter. Many Windows "desktop" applications which have a GUI (Graphical User Interface) call in console applications in the background to perform major tasks.

CMD Window

Console programs can run within the "Windows Command Processor" (CMD window) and are started using the "Command Prompt," also known as the "Command Language Interpreter (CLI)," and "Command-Line Interface." Because ML64 is a console program, we will use the "Windows Command Processor" (CMD window) for compiling and testing. The easiest way to start this command window is to enter CMD followed by the Enter key in the "search" box on the Windows task bar.

To arrive at the desired working directory for the example programs in this book, the following three commands should be entered in the command window:

- C:
- CD \ASM64
- DIR

Only the CD (Change Directory) command should be needed, but the other two commands won't hurt to be included. The first line should not be needed because the CMD processor will usually default to your C directory. The third line produces a directory which should show both the KERNEL32.LIB file and assembler source code files already run. Of course, these commands can be entered in lower case as well.

Path command

If you enter ML64 in the command window to start the assembler, you may get the following error response if a Path command has not been executed:

'ML64' is not recognized as an internal or external command, operable program or batch file.

The assembler and linker are not special Windows CMD processor commands, but console programs just like the ones we will be building. The CMD processor must be told where they are located, so we must first find them, and then set a "path" to them. Chapter 2 shows how to search for the locations of ML64.EXE and KERNEL32.LIB. .

path C:\######\Hostx64\x64;%PATH%

The above path statement consists of the word "path" followed by the file location containing the ML64 assembler, followed by a semicolon, and finally %PATH%. The file location will vary from computer to computer (that's why we searched for it), but it will probably begin with "C:\Program Files (x86)\Microsoft Visual Studio" and end with "\Hostx64\x64" (I have shown the middle as a series of # hash tags). The semicolon followed by %PATH% enables the new path to be included with any previous paths, but not replace them.

Rather than typing in the path command each time, I recommend putting it in a file with a name like masmpath.bat. Then, whenever you start the command window, just enter "masmpath" in response to the command prompt, and it will then substitute the path command.

ML64 Command Line

Listing B.1 shows the assembler producing one object file from one source code file. Typically, multiple files are assembled at the same time, and the linker can be called in as well.

```
C:\ASM64>ML64 /c main.asm
Microsoft (R) Macro Assembler (x64) Version
14.11.25547.0
Copyright (C) Microsoft Corporation. All rights reserved.

Assembling: main.asm

C:\ASM64>
```

Listing B.1: Assembling one file from command line

Listing B.2 shows the output of the ML64 help command. Some of the most common options include the /Fl "listing file" followed by the /link command and its options.

```
C:\ASM64>ML64 /help
Microsoft (R) Macro Assembler (x64) Version 14.11.25547.0
Copyright (C) Microsoft Corporation. All rights reserved.

   ML64 [/options ] filelist [/link linkoptions ]

/Bl<linker> Use alternate linker          /Sf Generate first pass listing
/c Assemble without linking               /Sl<width> Set line width
/Cp Preserve case of user identifiers     /Sn Suppress symbol-table listing
/Cx Preserve case in publics, externs     /Sp<length> Set page length
/D<name>[=text] Define text macro         /Ss<string> Set subtitle
/EP Output preprocessed listing to stdout /St<string> Set title
/F <hex> Set stack size (bytes)           /Sx List false conditionals
/Fe<file> Name executable                 /Ta<file> Assemble non-.ASM file
/Fl[file] Generate listing                /w Same as /W0 /WX
/Fm[file] Generate map                    /WX Treat warnings as errors
/Fo<file> Name object file                /W<number> Set warning level
/Fr[file] Generate limited browser info   /X Ignore INCLUDE environment path
/FR[file] Generate full browser info      /Zd Add line number debug info
/I<name> Add include path                 /Zf Make all symbols public
/link <linker options and libraries>      /Zi Add symbolic debug info
/nologo Suppress copyright message        /Zp[n] Set structure alignment
/Sa Maximize source listing               /Zs Perform syntax check only
/ZH:SHA_256 Use SHA256 for checksum
   in debug info (experimental)
/Gy[-] separate functions for linker
/errorReport:<option> Report internal assembler errors to Microsoft
   none - do not send report
   prompt - prompt to immediately send report
   queue - at next admin logon, prompt to send report
   send - send report automatically
```

Listing B.2: List of ML64 options and files

Batch Files

There are many ways to reduce keystrokes in command line processing. The easiest is to use the up-arrow key to repeat a previously entered line. A more powerful technique involves making a Windows Batch File (text file with .BAT file name extension).

If I have a file named MP . BAT containing the following one line, all I have to do is enter MP on the command line prompt to set the path to the directory containing the assembler and linker (as describe in Chapter 2).

path C:\Program Files (x86)\Microsoft Visual Studio\2017\
      Community\VC\Tools\MSVC\14.11.25503\bin\Hostx64\x64;%PATH%

Parameters can also be passed to a batch file. It is very similar to macro processing except the percent sign indicates each parameter (separated by one or more blanks). The first parameter will be substituted whenever %1 appears in the .BAT file, the second for %2, etc. If a file named MASM . BAT contains the following one line, then entering "MASM TEST" will assemble, list, and link the program in file TEST.asm.

ML64   /Fl%1.lst %1.asm   /link   /SUBSYSTEM:CONSOLE   /ENTRY:main

Multiple parameters can also be entered. For example, the following M . BAT file can assemble up to four assembler files and link them. Entering "M main.asm   v_asc.asm" will assemble two files and link them. The third and fourth parameters are blank.

ML64   %1   %2   %3
       %4   /link   /SUBSYSTEM:CONSOLE   /ENTRY:main

Appendix C
List of Instructions

Appendix C provides a list of X86-64 instructions and assembler directives used in programming examples in this book. The first column in each of the following tables contains a three number field indicating the chapter, listing number, and text line number where the instruction is first used. For example, 3.5.27 indicates the instruction is on line 27 of Listing 5 in Chapter 3. Other instructions and directives are also described in this book and can most easily be located through the Table of Contents.

2.4.6.	add	RCX,100	; Immediate add to contents of RCX
7.1.18.	and	AL,1	; Mask off all bits except bit 0.
2.1.6.	call	ExitProcess	; Return CPU control to Windows
7.1.11.	cld		; String instructions will increment.
4.1.57.	cmp	R8,2	; Test if only CR and LF characters.
4.3.63.	dec	R13	; Decrement remaining byte count.
8.1.18.	div	R11B	; Get quotient in AL, remainder in AH.
4.3.62.	inc	R12	; Set pointer to next character.
4.1.58.	jg	nxtlin	; Loop back around for next input.
7.1.22.	jge	nxtbit	; Continue until all 8 bits done.
3.1.21.	lea	RDX,msg	; Pointer to message (byte array).
9.1.60.	lodsb		; Load next byte and inc RSI.
9.4.60.	lodsq		; Load next quad and inc RSI.
9.3.60.	lodsw		; Load next word and inc RSI.
2.1.5.	mov	RCX,78	; Load exit status code into RCX
9.8.61.	mov	R12,[R13+8*R15]	; Load next quad.
9.6.60.	movsq		; Copy next quad and inc RSI,RDI.
10.1.64.	or	R13,qword ptr [cvt]	; Convert to lower case.
7.1.30.	pop	RDI	; Reload RDI and reposition stack.
7.1.8.	push	RDI	; Save RDI and decrement RSP by 8
9.7.60.	rep	movsq	; Copy block of memory.
5.3.88.	ret		; Return to the calling program.
7.1.17.	shr	AL,CL	; Shift current bit to bit 0.
7.1.20.	stosb		; Store in array of 8 "bits."
9.3.61.	stosw		; Store word from AX and inc RDI.
2.4.8.	sub	RCX,RDX	; Subtract register RDX from RCX
7.4.18.	xlat		; Convert 4-bit nibble to hex digit
10.1.58.	xor	R13,qword ptr [cvt]	; "Flip" the letter case.

Listing C.1: Program location for first appearance of X86 instructions

12.1.7.	addps	XMM0,XMM1	; Add Pi to argument.
11.1.57.	movdqu	XMM8,xmmword ptr [keymsg]	; First 16 bytes of message.
12.1.6.	movups	XMM1,pi	; Load floating point Pi value.
11.3.48.	paddb	XMM3,XMM3	; Double the value in XMM3.
11.3.50.	paddsb	XMM3,XMM3	; Signed Saturated values in XMM3.
11.3.49.	paddusb	XMM3,XMM3	; Unsigned Saturated values in XMM3
11.1.64.	por	XMM8,xmmword ptr [cvt]	; Convert to lower case.
11.1.58.	pxor	XMM8,xmmword ptr [cvt]	; "Flip" the letter case.

Listing C.2: Program location for first appearance of SSE instructions

9.1.78.	align	16	
3.1.33. msg	byte	"Hello World"	
2.1.3.	.code		
3.1.32.	.data		
7.1.35. bits8	byte	8 **DUP** (?)	; Memory buffer for display
2.1.8.	end		
5.1.19.	endm		
2.1.7. main	endp		
3.1.4. Console	equ	-11	; Device code for console text output.
2.1.1.	includelib	kernel32.lib	
3.1.22.	mov	R8,**lengthof** msg	; Number of characters to display
5.1.13. msgOut	macro	msg	; One argument: msg
2.1.4. main	proc		; Program external name
2.1.2. ExitProcess	proto		
12.1.12. pi	real4	3.1416	; Approximate value of Pi
3.1.34. stdout	qword	?	; Handle to standard output device

Listing C.3: Program location for first appearance of assembler directives

Obviously, not all X86-64 instructions nor assembler directives are represented in this book. There are many very good technical reference manuals available on the Internet that provide tables of all possible instructions and directives.

Appendix D
X64 Calling Convention

Functions are entered simply by executing the "machine code" CALL instruction, which saves the current RIP instruction pointer on the run-time stack and then sets the RIP to the first instruction of the function. However, all "called" functions, including Windows Application Program Interface (API) functions, C++ functions, and subroutines, must be told what to do, and that is done using software calling conventions. The parameters needed, such as which device to read and write as well as how much data is to be transferred, is passed in "arguments."

In 32-bit Windows, there were several "standards" for passing arguments, but in 64-bit Windows, only the X64 Calling Convention (summarized below) is used to call the Windows API functions and C functions.

1. Return Address: The last 64-bit value pushed onto the run-time stack (register RSP) contains the address of the instruction to be executed after the function is finished.
2. Location of arguments: The first four arguments are passed in registers. Integer arguments (including characters and memory addresses) are in RCX, RDX, R8, and R9. Floating point values are in XMM0 through XMM3. If more than four arguments, then they will be pushed onto the stack (see following Table D.1).
3. Function Return Value: Integer functions return their results in RAX, while floating point functions return their results in XMM0, Void functions (a.k.a., subroutines) do not return a value.
4. Run-time Stack Alignment: The RSP register must be on a 16-byte (128 bits) memory address boundary (i.e., the lower 4 bits of RSP must be zero).
5. Shadow space: Preceding the return address on the run-time stack, there will be at least 32 bytes of "scratch" space that the called function can use if it chooses. This is enough space to store the contents of the first four arguments. Because the CALL instruction pushes its return address (8 bytes) onto the stack, a shadow space of 40 bytes is typically reserved on the stack before each function call in order to meet both the storage and alignment requirements.
6. Volatile registers: The calling program assumes registers RAX, RCX, RDX, R8 through R11, and XMM0 through XMM5 are volatile (i.e., they will be modified and not saved by the function). The contents of registers RBX, RSI, RDI, RBP, RSP, R12 through R15, and XMM6 through XMM15 are considered non-volatile (i.e., they will have the

same contents on return from the function as when the function was called).

Argument Number	Integer	Floating Point
1	RCX	XMM0
2	RDX	XMM1
3	R8	XMM2
4	R9	XMM3
5	[RSP + 40]	
6	[RSP + 48]	
N	[RSP + 8 * N]	
Return	RAX	XMM0

Table D.1: Argument location for integers and floating point

Value or Reference

Each argument passed to a function is either a value (integer, floating point, or character) or a pointer to a value (memory address):

1. Pass by value: The argument is contained in the register or on the stack. Integer and single character (char) values are passed in registers RCX, RDX, R8, and R9. Floating point values are passed in registers XMM0 through XMM3.
2. Pass by reference: The argument value is in memory and is pointed to by an address either in a register or on the stack. In the C language, an ampersand (&) before a variable name indicates "memory address of" rather than "value of" a variable. Arrays and character strings (char[]) are passed by reference. Floating point reference addresses are passed in registers RCX, RDX, R8, and R9, not XMM0 through XMM3.

example (10, 20.1, &intParm, &floatparm, 100, &intParm)

1. RCX contains integer value 10
2. XMM1 contains floating point 20.1
3. R8 contains reference address of variable intParm
4. R9 contains reference address of variable floatParm
5. [RSP + 40] memory location contains integer value 100
6. [RSP + 48] memory location contains address of variable intParm

Appendix E
Windows API Function Calls

One of the main responsibilities of an operating system, such as Windows, is to provide services for application programs. A large portion of these services consists of functions for reading and writing peripheral devices (display monitor, keyboard, mouse, network, etc.) and disk files (real spinning disks as well as solid-state memory devices). The calling program must provide Windows with the details of what is to be performed:

1. What is to be done
2. Which device is to written or read
3. Where the data buffer is in the program's memory
4. How much data is to be written or read

	List of Windows function calls introduced in this book
ExitProcess	Terminate the program.
GetStdHandle	Get console program standard device handle.
ReadConsoleA	Read ASCII bytes from device into memory buffer
ReadConsoleW	Read Unicode 16-bit words from device into memory buffer
WriteConsoleA	Write array of ASCII bytes to device from memory buffer
WriteConsoleW	Write array of Unicode words to device from memory buffer

Table E.1: Windows functions for read/write console applications

ExitProcess: Terminate program

An application program starts when Windows gives it control at its /Entry label, and when a program chooses to quit, it will return control back to Windows by calling ExitProcess.

5.	mov	RCX,78	; Load exit status code into RCX
6.	call	ExitProcess	; Return CPU control to Windows

Listing E.1: Example from Chapter 2 to quit program

Standard Device Handles

There are three standard character I/O devices associated with the "Console Program" command window. The device *stdin* refers to the standard character input stream that by default is the keyboard, but can be redirected to an alternate device or file. A second standard device name is *stdout* which by default is the display monitor, but can be redirected to an alternate device or file. A third standard device name is *stderr*, which is by default the same as *stdout*, but can be redirected to a file.

Before text data can be written to or read from the command window, the device must be identified, opened, and assigned a "handle" (ID number) by calling "GetStdHandle" using one of the following codes in register RCX, The handle ID number returned in RAX will be used for all subsequent data transfers.

1. STD_INPUT_HANDLE, -10
2. STD_OUTPUT_HANDLE, -11
3. STD_ERROR_HANDLE, -12

| 20. | mov | RCX,-11 | ; Console standard output handle |
| 21. | call | GetStdHandle | ; Returns handle in register RAX |

Listing E.2: Example from Chapter 3 to get standard output handle

ReadConsoleA: Read Data from Keyboard Buffer

Reading from the keyboard involves first obtaining the standard input device handle, and then using either ReadConsoleA for ASCII input or ReadConsoleW for Unicode input.

call ReadConsoleA (4 arguments):

1. RCX: Value of "handle"
2. RDX: Reference pointing to memory buffer to receive the data
3. R8: Value of the maximum number of characters to be read.
4. R9: Reference points to 64-bit memory location to receive number of bytes actually written.

The character count returned to memory location pointed to by R9 may be less than the value provided in register R8, but will not be more.

37.	mov	RCX,stdin	; Handle to standard input device
38.	mov	R8,20	; Maximum length to receive
39.	lea	RDX,keymsg	; Memory address to receive input
40.	lea	R9,nbrd	; Number of bytes actually read.
41.	call	ReadConsoleA	; Read text string from command box.

Listing E.3: Example from Chapter 3 to read ASCII characters from keyboard

WriteConsoleA: Write Text Data Data to I/O Command Window

Unless redirected to a file or another device, WriteConsoleA will write ASCII characters to the command window for *stdout* and *stderr* devices. The four registers and their meaning for the WriteConsoleA function are as follows:

1. RCX: Register containing value of handle from opening either *stdout* or *stderr*
2. RDX: Register pointing to memory buffer containing the data
3. R8: Register holding the number of characters to be written
4. R9: Reference points to memory address to receive 64-bit count of characters actually written

45.	mov	RCX,stdout	; Handle to standard output device
46.	lea	RDX,keymsg	; Pointer to message that was input
47.	mov	R8,nbrd	; Length (bytes) of input message
48.	lea	R9,nbwr	; Number of bytes actually written.
49.	call	WriteConsoleA	; Write text string to command box.

Listing E.4: Example from Chapter 3 to write to display monitor

The character count returned to memory location pointed to by R9 may be less than the value provided in register R8, but will not be more. If WriteConsoleA is used, the data has to be ASCII encoded characters in byte array, while if WriteConsoleW is used the data must be Unicode encoded in a word array.

File Handles

The techniques presented in this book for reading and writing to the command window are very similar to those used for file I/O. I recommend looking into the following list of Windows API functions. Please search docs.microsoft.com. These functions will primarily be described related to C or C++ programs, but that is simply the same as the X64 Calling Convention.

	List of some Windows function related to file I/O
CreateFileA	Open a new or existing "disk" file
ReadFileA	Read block of bytes from opened file
WriteFileA	Write memory array to opened file
SetFilePointer	Define "disk" position for next read or write
CloseHandle	Close handle created by CreateFileA
DeleteFileA	Delete file from directory
FindFirstFileA	Examine directory for file (usually with wild cards)

Table E.2: Windows API functions for file I/O

In the above list there is a Unicode 16-bit API function corresponding to each ASCII 8-bit data API function. Actually, Windows converts the ASCII to Unicode functions, such as CreateFileA to CreateFileW. C programmers should simply use CreateFile, and let the compiler generate either CreateFileA or CreateFileW based upon the data type.

There is also an OpenFile function for opening existing files, but it should not be used for new applications. The CreateFile function should be used for both new as well as opening existing files.

Appendix F
ASCII

Why ASCII? Why not Baudot, BCD, Display Code, Fieldata, Unicode, XS3, or any other character code?

What is a Character Code

Binary computers store and manipulate bits (binary digits). Numbers are represented by "groups of bits" as either integers or real numbers. That's fine for science and engineering applications, but what's stored in "groups of bits" for business applications, such as correspondence, reports, and mailing lists? How is this text data consisting of letters, digits, and punctuation represented by "groups of bits"? A character code is a set that assigns each text character to a unique number.

This was not so much of a problem 3000 years ago. Several of the ancient languages including Assyrian, Hebrew, and Greek were "computer ready," but our modern written languages, such as English, are not. In these ancient languages, every symbol used to compose words was also used to compose numbers. The symbols alpha and beta in Greek were assigned both sounds to form words as well as numeric values to write numbers. In English, letters and digits are separate (i.e., the letter "R" does not have a numeric value). This means there was no "standard" for storing text data as a series of numbers.

In the 1960s, several companies were manufacturing mainframe computer systems. They were competing for sales and were interested in locking customers into their unique designs rather than making computer data files and applications portable from one system to another. There were basically two problems with character codes in the 1960s:

- Each character was stored in a byte, but the number of bits composing a byte varied from system to system.
- Each character was assigned a unique numeric code, but each computer system had a different set of character code assignments..

Several mainframe computer systems had 6-bit bytes, which supported a set of 64 different characters. BCD, Display Code, Fieldata, and XS3 are examples of 6-bit codes. Each of these sets contained 26 upper case letters, 10 digits, and a few punctuation marks and control characters. In order to include lower case letters, IBM switched from a 6-bit code to an 8-bit EBCDIC code in the mid 1960s. The size of the byte determines how many different characters can be represented as listed below:

- 6 bits: 64 characters
- 7 bits: 128 characters
- 8 bits: 256 characters
- 16 bits: 65,536 characters

The second compatibility problem was that the unique assignments were inconsistent among the different character code sets and computer systems. It took a presidential decree to alleviate some of the inconsistencies. On March 11, 1968, President Johnson signed ASCII (American Standard Code for Information Interchange) into existence.

Character Code	Letter A	Digit 5	blank
IBM BCD	11	05	30
CDC Display Code	01	20	2D
Univac Fieldata	06	25	05
XS3	14	08	33
EBCDIC	C1	F5	40
ASCII	41	33	20
Unicode	41	33	20

Table F.1: Example of three characters expressed in various character codes (in hexadecimal)

The 7-bit ASCII code from 1968 was fine for the English language, but it could not even support all the characters used in French, Spanish, and other Latin languages. In 1985, character set ISO 8859 was defined as an 8-bit code with 256 character codes defined, where the first 128 are identical to 7-bit ASCII. The remaining 128 character codes were assigned to accent characters for the Latin languages and a variety of special symbols like copyright and trademark.

Hex Code	Symbol	Hex Code	Symbol	Hex Code	Symbol
30	0	40	@	50	P
31	1	41	A	51	Q
32	2	42	B	52	R
33	3	43	C	53	S
34	4	44	D	54	T
35	5	45	E	55	U
36	6	46	F	56	V
37	7	47	G	57	W
38	8	48	H	58	X
39	9	49	I	59	Y
3A	:	4A	J	5A	Z
3B	;	4B	K	5B	[
3C	<	4C	L	5C	\
3D	=	4D	M	5D	]
3E	>	4E	N	5E	^
3F	?	4F	O	5F	_

Table F.2: ASCII and ISO codes in hexadecimal

Hex Code	Symbol	Hex Code	Symbol	Hex Code	Symbol
60	`	70	p		
61	a	71	q		
62	b	72	r		
63	c	73	s		
64	d	74	t		
65	e	75	u		
66	f	76	v		
67	g	77	w		
68	h	78	x		
69	i	79	y		
6A	j	7A	z		
6B	k	7B	{		
6C	l	7C				
6D	m	7D	}		
6E	n	7E	~		
6F	o	7F				

Table F.3: ASCII and ISO codes in hexadecimal

What about those written languages like Hebrew and Greek that were "computer ready" thousands of years ago? Were they still computer ready in 1968 when ASCII was defined? They were by themselves, but to include them alongside ASCII and ISO 8895, a new character set has been defined: Unicode. Casually speaking, Unicode is considered to be a 16-bit code supporting 65,536 different character code symbols, enough to encompass all the written symbols composing thousands of different languages. The first 128 characters of Unicode are the same as the ASCII character set.

Appendix G
Binary Numbers

To be precise, it's not the numbers that are binary, but the written representation of numbers. For example, we currently count eight planets in the solar system. This has been "written down" as 8, VIII, 10_8, 1000_2, as well as a variety of other representations throughout history.

What's Binary?

Binary means *two* like a binary star system consisting of a pair of stars. In the case of binary "numbers," the *two* refers to the base, also known as the radix, which indicates how many different symbols (or digits) can be used. In our every day decimal (base 10) system, there are ten symbols available {0, 1, 2, 3, 4, 5, 6, 7, 8, 9} so we can represent a number in a form like 3274, 1620, and 36. While in binary (base 2), we have only two symbols available {0, 1} so we are restricted to representing numbers in a form like 1100, 10101, 1, and 111. Other popular bases that have been used in the computer industry are octal (base 8) having eight symbols {0, 1, 2, 3, 4, 5, 6, 7} and hexadecimal (base 16) having sixteen symbols {0, 1, 2, 3, 4, 5, 6, 7, 8, 9, A, B, C, D, E, F}.

Why Binary?

The simple answer is that the logical building blocks (i.e., electronics in today's systems) are simpler and more efficient in binary than they are in our everyday decimal. The electronic logic circuits have two states: High and Low (voltage levels) which can model a variety of binary states like True and False, Yes and No, and of course One and Zero. This system follows the logic attributed to Aristotle thousands of years ago.

In the following table, we compare the written representations of counting from 0 to 12 in five different bases. Notice how the rightmost column (one's place) is incremented through all of the possible symbols available in the base before the next column to its left is incremented.

base 10 10 symbols {0123456789}	base 2 2 symbols {01}	base 3 3 symbols {012}	base 4 4 symbols {0123}	base 5 5 symbols {01234}
0	0	0	0	0
1	1	1	1	1
2	10	2	2	2
3	11	10	3	3
4	100	11	10	4
5	101	12	11	10
6	110	20	12	11
7	111	21	13	12
8	1000	22	20	13
9	1001	100	21	14
10	1010	101	22	20
11	1011	102	23	21
12	1100	110	30	22

Table G.1: Counting from 0 to 12 in bases 10, 2, 3, 4, and 5

Column	3	2	1	0
Base 10	$10^3=1000$	$10^2=100$	$10^1=10$	$10^0=1$
Base 2	$2^3=8$	$2^2=4$	$2^1=2$	$2^0=1$
Base 3	$3^3=27$	$3^2=9$	$3^1=3$	$3^0=1$
Base 4	$4^3=64$	$4^2=16$	$4^1=4$	$4^0=1$
Base 5	$5^3=125$	$5^2=25$	$5^1=5$	$5^0=1$

Table G.2: Value of each column in bases 10, 2, 3, 4, and 5

The Problems with Binary

The problems with binary are not with computers, but with us humans:

1. We are comfortable with base ten and have used it daily for most of our lives.
2. Binary numbers are awkward for us due to the large number of columns required. Who would prefer replacing the decimal representation of 7094, 1620, 1108, 6600, 3033, and 7800 with their binary equivalents 1101110110110, 11001010100, 10001010100, 1100111001000, 101111011001, and 1111001111000?
3. Conversion between binary and decimal is difficult to do "in our

heads." The difficulty stems from the fact that 10 is not an integer power of two.

Superscripts and Subscripts

In math books, the base (or radix) used to represent a number is given as a subscript. For example: a number written in decimal would be like 257_{10} and in binary it would be like 10000001_2. If no subscript is provided, we assume it is decimal unless it is stated in the text that the numbers are expressed in a different base such as binary. When working with computer programs, whether assembler or higher level, subscripts are not commonly available so binary is generally entered as 0b10101, 10101b, or %10101 depending on the computer system or application being used.

Superscripts indicate a number raised to a power. For example, 4^3 means $4 \times 4 \times 4$ equaling 64 and 2^8 is $2 \times 2 \times 2 \times 2 \times 2 \times 2 \times 2 \times 2$ equaling 256. Also recall that 2^0, 10^0, 16^0, and any non-zero number raised to the zeroth power equals one.

A decimal number is really a short notation for a polynomial of powers of 10. For example: 137_{10} is $1 \times 10^2 + 3 \times 10^1 + 7 \times 10^0$ which is $100 + 30 + 7$. Likewise, a binary number is really a short notation for a polynomial of powers of 2. For example: 110101_2 is $1 \times 2^5 + 1 \times 2^4 + 0 \times 2^3 + 1 \times 2^2 + 0 \times 2^1 + 1 \times 2^0$. By the way, this polynomial structure is the main reason we label and count bits within a byte or word from right to left starting with zero.

Bit Position	3	2	1	0
Power of 2	$2^3=8$	$2^2=4$	$2^1=2$	$2^0=1$
Binary example	1	0	1	1
$1011_2 = 1 \times 2^3 + 0 \times 2^2 + 1 \times 2^1 + 1 \times 2^0 = 8 + 0 + 2 + 1 = 11_{10}$				

Table G.3: Bit position example: $1011_2 = 2^3 + 0 + 2^1 + 2^0 = 8 + 0 + 2 + 1 = 11_{10}$

Conversion to Any Base

A popular way to convert a number to a particular base is successive division. The remainders from each division will provide the digits (i.e., symbols) beginning with rightmost digit. For example, converting the number 3274 to decimal follows:

1. $3274 / 10 = 327$ Remainder 4
2. $327 / 10 = 32$ Remainder 7
3. $32 / 10 = 3$ Remainder 2
4. $3 / 10 = 0$ Remainder 3

So the "number" 3274 is represented in decimal as the sequence of remainders "3" "2" "7" and "4." By the way: This technique of successively dividing a number by the desired base works regardless of how the "computer" internally stores numbers. It could be binary, decimal, or any conceivable internal structure that would permit division.

Converting the same number 3274 to binary follows:

1. 3274 / 2 = 1637 Remainder 0
2. 1637 / 2 = 818 Remainder 1
3. 818 / 2 = 409 Remainder 0
4. 409 / 2 = 204 Remainder 1
5. 204 / 2 = 102 Remainder 0
6. 102 / 2 = 51 Remainder 0
7. 51 / 2 = 25 Remainder 1
8. 25 / 2 = 12 Remainder 1
9. 12 / 2 = 6 Remainder 0
10. 6 / 2 = 3 Remainder 0
11. 3 / 2 = 1 Remainder 1
12. 1 / 2 = 0 Remainder 1

So the "number" 3274 is represented in binary as the sequence of remainders "1" "1" "0" "0" "1" "1" "0" "0" "1" "0" "1" and "0." As an exercise, try converting 3274 to base five by successively dividing by five until the quotient is zero (3274/5 = 654 remainder 4, ...). The answer will be 101044_5.

Multiplying and Dividing by Shifting

If we want to multiply by ten "in our heads" in our everyday decimal system, we just append a zero. For example to multiply 709 by 10, we append "0" to "709" and get "7090." Likewise, when we multiply by 100 (i.e., 10^2), we append two zeroes, and for 1000, we append 3 zeroes, etc. For dividing by powers of ten, we do the reverse: we remove zeroes on the right. What if there are not enough zeros present on the right? Then we move the decimal point. For example to divide 1108 by 100, we move the decimal point to the left two places giving us 11.08.

When we shift a number to the left in base two, we are multiplying by a power of two, and when we shift to the right, we are dividing by a power of two. This means that conversion into and from binary format is done very efficiently using shifting rather than division. Converting the same number 3274 (110011001010_2) to binary by shifting is below. Note: The notation ">> 1" means shift 1 bit position to the right, and the "Carry out" refers to the rightmost bit that is lost when the value is shifted.

1. 110011001010 >> 1 = 11001100101 with Carry out 0
2. 11001100101 >> 1 = 1100110010 Carry out 1
3. 1100110010 >> 1 = 110011001 Carry out 0

4. 110011001 >> 1 = 11001100 Carry out 1
5. 11001100 >> 1 = 1100110 Carry out 0
6. 1100110 >> 1 = 110011 Carry out 0
7. 110011 >> 1 = 11001 Carry out 1
8. 11001 >> 1 = 1100 Carry out 1
9. 1100 >> 1 = 110 Carry out 0
10. 110 >> 1 = 11 Carry out 0
11. 11 >> 1 = 1 Carry out 1
12. 1 >> 1 = 0 Carry out 1

Converting Digits Into a Number

To convert "written digits" into a number, run the above process in reverse: Do successive multiplications. For example in base 10: the sequence of digits "1" "6" "2" "2" could be used to "build" the number 1622 as follows:

1. Start with 0
2. $0 \times 10 + 1 = 1$
3. $1 \times 10 + 6 = 16$
4. $16 \times 10 + 2 = 162$
5. $162 \times 10 + 2 = 1622$

In binary, it is simply a matter of shifting to the left one bit position to "multiply" by two. In the following example, the number expressed as a sequence of digits "110011001010" is built by a series of logical left shifts notated by "<< 1" combined with a logical OR notated by "+":

1. Start with 0
2. 0 << 1 + 1 = 1
3. 1 << 1 + 1 = 11
4. 11 << 1 + 0 = 110
5. 110 << 1 + 0 = 1100
6. 1100 << 1 + 1 = 11001
7. 11001 << 1 + 1 = 110011
8. 110011 << 1 + 0 = 1100110
9. 1100110 << 1 + 0 = 11001100
10. 11001100 << 1 + 1 = 110011001
11. 110011001 << 1 + 0 = 1100110010
12. 1100110010 << 1 + 1 = 11001100101
13. 11001100101 << 1 + 0 = 110011001010

Negative Binary Numbers

When we include negative numbers, we effectively double how many numbers we have to be able to represent in binary. For every positive number, we have a corresponding negative number. This requires an additional bit, a "sign" bit, that has to be associated with every binary number in registers and storage.

Rather than append an additional bit to each numeric storage type, computer manufacturers have chosen to steal a bit from the positive range. Instead of an 8-bit byte supporting numbers in the range of 0 through 255, it supports -128 through +127 for "signed" bytes. Likewise, signed half-words have a range of -32,768 to +32,767 rather than 0 through 65,535 for the unsigned format. The range is actually the same, but it has been shifted by 50%.

There have been four formats popular for representing signed numbers in binary computers:

- **Bias:** Add ½ the total range to all numbers
- **Sign and magnitude:** High order (leftmost) bit is the sign: 1 for negative
- **One's complement:** Complement (i.e., toggle) all bits for negative.
- **Two's complement:** Add 1 to one's complement value

The question is, which one is popular in today's computers? Being even more specific, which are present in the X86-64 architecture? Three are used: two's complement represents signed integers in the X86 CPU while both sign/magnitude and bias are used in the floating point format available in the SSE and AVX extensions. Table G.4 gives 8-bit binary examples where positive and negative 26_{10} are represented four ways. I've also included zero, including the rather unexpected negative zero case.

Decimal	+ 26	− 26	+ 0	− 0
Sign & Magnitude	00011010	10011010	00000000	10000000
One's Complement	00011010	11100101	00000000	11111111
Two's Complement	00011010	11100110	00000000	00000000
Biased	10011010	01100110	10000000	10000000

Table G.4: Comparison of +26, –26, +0, and –0 in four signed byte formats

Nine's complement

How can we subtract using an "adding machine"? This question was not new with electronic computers, but goes back to the days when accountants and human "computers" used mechanical adding machines. It involves converting the algebraic expression "A – B" to "A + (–B)" which transforms the question into how should we represent –B?

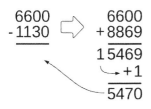

Accountants, working in base ten, could represent a negative number by subtracting each of its digits from nine (one less than the base). On the left, we see an example where the negative of 1130 is 8869 in nine's complement (each 8 comes from 9 – 1, the 6 comes from 9 – 3, and the 9 comes from 9 – 0).

Figure G.1: Nine's complement example of subtraction by addition

Obviously, since we're adding, rather than subtracting, the result is larger than we want, but if you do the algebra, you'll notice that the correct answer can be achieved. Notice how the first sum in Figure G.1 had a "carry out" that did not fit in the number of columns we were using. If you add this carry in a second step as shown, the correct answer appears. If there is no carry, do not add it, and there will be a large number, but it is really a negative number.

One's complement

One's complement is the same as nine's complement except the base is now two: every digit is subtracted from 1, instead of 9. Actually, this technique works in any base. Do the algebra if you like to prove it. Because there's only two symbols in base 2, one's complement is achieved by simply inverting each bit as is shown in Figure G.2.

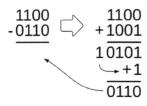

Figure G.2: One's complement
example of subtraction by addition

Just like in nine's complement a subtraction is converted into an addition. Here the negative of "0110" is calculated to be "1001" where the value in each column is calculated by subtracting it from one less than the base. Notice that it's still a two-step process where the carry out is added back to obtain the correct answer.

If you follow the above naming convention, you would think that two's complement involves numbers expressed in base 3. Actually, the expression "two's complement" refers to the technique that eliminates the second step during a subtraction.

Two's complement

In two's complement, the negative of a number is generated by adding one to the one's complement and ignoring any caries. For example, the negative of 0110 is $1001 + 1 = 1010$.

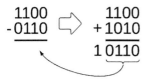

Figure G.3: Two's complement
example of subtraction by addition

Rather than adding the "carry out" as a second step, a 1-bit is added preemptively when the negative is generated. Then during the subtraction, the carry is just ignored, making two's complement subtractions twice as fast as one's complement subtractions.

Appendix H
Hexadecimal Numbers

To be precise, it's not the numbers that are hexadecimal, but the written representation of numbers. Hexadecimal is a compact form of binary representation where we have sixteen symbols {0,1,2,3,4,5,6,7,8,9,A,B,C,D,E,F} to represent numbers. If you're not familiar with binary representation, please read Appendix B before studying hexadecimal. If it wasn't for binary, there would be negligible need for hexadecimal in the computer industry.

A decimal number is really a short notation for a polynomial of powers of 10. For example: 137_{10} is $1 \times 10^2 + 3 \times 10^1 + 7 \times 10^0$ which is $100 + 30 + 7$. Likewise, a binary number is really a short notation for a polynomial of powers of 2. For example: 110101_2 is $1 \times 2^5 + 1 \times 2^4 + 0 \times 2^3 + 1 \times 2^2 + 0 \times 2^1 + 1 \times 2^0$. A hexadecimal number is really a short notation for a polynomial of powers of 16. For example: $5A732C_{16}$ is $5 \times 16^5 + 10 \times 16^4 + 7 \times 16^3 + 3 \times 16^2 + 2 \times 16^1 + 12 \times 16^0$ where A and C are digits representing values of 10 and 12, respectively.

Why Use Hexadecimal?

The simple answer is hexadecimal is compact, and it is very easy for us humans to convert between binary and hexadecimal. Consider the following:

1. Internally, almost all our computer systems are based in binary (see Lab 5 and Appendix B for an explanation).
2. Inputting and displaying numbers in the computer's natural binary notation is very efficient for the computer, but clumsy and inefficient for us humans. Who is comfortable reading and entering numbers like 100001101010010 or 1101101101101, and even much longer ones up to 64 bits in length?
3. Decimal is a rather compact form of representing numbers, and we are very comfortable with it because we use it in our daily lives. We can convert between decimal and binary by using successive divisions by ten. However, that is slow and cumbersome to do "in our heads." A division by sixteen is simply a four bit shift, but a division by ten cannot be achieved by shifting bits.
4. Do we humans actually need to use binary? As people working with computers at a detailed architectural level, we have to see the actual bits. We have to look at status words, IP addresses, instruction formats, and memory dumps.

Table H.1 shows counting from 0 to 17 in decimal, binary, hexadecimal, and octal. Notice how one hexadecimal digit fits exactly in four bits. Figure H.1 shows a binary number being "mapped" to hexadecimal digits, four bits at a time. starting from the right side.

base 10 10 symbols {0123456789}	base 2 2 symbols {01}	base 16 16 symbols {0123456789ABCDEF}	base 8 8 symbols {01234567}
0	0	0	0
1	1	1	1
2	10	2	2
3	11	3	3
4	100	4	4
5	101	5	5
6	110	6	6
7	111	7	7
8	1000	8	10
9	1001	9	11
10	1010	A	12
11	1011	B	13
12	1100	C	14
13	1101	D	15
14	1110	E	16
15	1111	F	17
16	10000	10	20
17	10001	11	21

Table H.1: Counting from 0 to 17 in four different bases

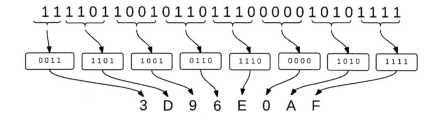

Figure H.1: Convert binary to hex, 4 bits at a time starting from the right (low order) side

Answers to
Selected Questions

Questions marked with an asterisk (*) in the Review Questions and Programming Exercises section of each chapter have their answers, or at least hints, provided below.

1.4 "By hand, without a calculator or computer," convert the following numbers expressed in decimal to binary format. See Appendix G if you need some background in binary.

      a. $21_{10} = 10101_2$
      b. $63_{10} = 111111_2$
      c. $16_{10} = 10000_2$
      d. $129_{10} = 10000001_2$

1.5 "By hand, without a calculator or computer," convert the following numbers expressed in binary to decimal format. See Appendix G if you need some background in binary.

      a. $1011_2 = 11_{10}$
      b. $1100101_2 = 101_{10}$
      c. $10110_2 = 22_{10}$
      d. $100001_2 = 33_{10}$
      e. $1111011_2 = 123_{10}$

2.5 When updating a line of source code, should the comment on the line be updated as well?

      Yes, usually. However, sometimes the comment is right, but the code was wrong. For example, the comment said why the line of code was present, but the code did not work. The worst case is when someone changed what the code was supposed to be doing, but left the old comment which is now irrelevant and much worse than no comment at all.

3.3 In the C language, a "function" is an extension of a "procedure" that allows the return of a single value associated with the function, such as Y = SQRT(X). Where do you think the return value is located within the X64 Calling Convention?

Register RAX

3.7 The 40 bytes of shadow space meets the requirements for alignment and room to store four 64-bit registers. What else is assumed to make this value of 40 work for the alignment requirement in particular?

It is assumed that the RSP is already aligned to a 128-bit (16 bytes) memory location when the program is started and a subroutine is called. Otherwise, adding 40 bytes would not create alignment. Alignment could, of course, be achieved with an AND instruction, but then the incoming RSP value would also have to be saved somewhere (i.e., several instructions instead of just one).

4.7. On lines 63 and 64 of Listing 4.3, a DEC followed by a JG is used to continue the loop. Why wasn't a LOOP instruction used instead?

A first answer is that the LOOP instruction is very specific and restrictive: The CX register is decremented, and if the result is greater than zero, it jumps back to continue the loop. I wanted the loop to continue until negative, not just zero. But even more important is that CX is volatile according to the X64 calling Convention, and it would have mostly likely been changed by the call to the Windows function. Also, in many X86-64 processors, the LOOP instruction actually runs a little slower than the combined DEC and JG,

5.2. How is a macro different from a subroutine?

- A macro is called while the assembler is running, and a subroutine is called when the application program (being written) is running.
- A macro generates text lines that will later be "assembled," while a subroutine works with numbers and text of the running application.
- Each macro call makes the program physically larger and take up more memory, while subroutines generally reduce memory requirements by eliminating duplicate code.

5.3. Give an example of a useful macro that generates neither any instructions nor any data.

Just a few examples are listed below:

- ALIGN statement to indicate a word or double word boundary will be used next.
- EQU statements to assign values to constants used at assembly time.
- .CODE or .DATA to indicate where following instructions and data are to be placed.

5.4. What is a principal danger in using "pass by reference"?

One of the hallmarks of object oriented programming is "information hiding." If a part of a program does not need access to a part of the data, don't give it access. "Pass by reference" provides the location of the data to the subroutine, and if the subroutine makes a mistake, it can write over the original source of the data. In "pass by value," only a copy of the original data is sent as an argument to a subroutine. Of course, if all programs and subroutines worked perfectly, none of this would be a concern.

6.3. If you were going to build a library named "engines.lib" from three object files named "electric.obj," "gasoline.obj," and "diesel.obj," what command line would be needed?

LIB   /out : engines.lib   /verbose   electric.obj   gasoline.obj diesel.obj

6.4. What assembler directive would be used to find the "engines.lib" library built in question 3?

includelib   engines.lib

7.2. Even though subroutine v_asc does not fully abide by the X64 Calling Convention, why must the RSP stack pointer be 16-byte aligned by the push instruction on line 8 of subroutine v_bin in Listing 7.1?

Subroutine v_asc needs the RSP aligned on a 16-byte boundary when it calls the Windows API WriteConsoleA which is fully compliant with the X64 Calling Convention.

7.4. Octal was a very popular base used in assembly language for many years because it is also a compact form for expressing binary numbers. Although still available, why has hexadecimal almost universally replaced it?

> Basically, the size of a "byte" changed from 6 bits to 8 bits. In the 1960s and 1970s, most mainframes and mini-computers used 6-bit character codes supporting only 64 characters. Lower case letters were generally not available. Octal converts a 3-bit binary number into an octal digit in the range of 0 through 7. A 6-bit value can be converted into two octal digits, while three octal digits are required to express an 8-bit value. Hexadecimal, although looking awkward by having 0 through 9 mixed with A through F, is a better fit for expressing multiples of 8 bits.

8,2. The overflow flag sometimes indicates an error occurred and sometimes it doesn't. Why doesn't the CPU know for sure if there is an error? Hint: See Appendix G.

> A great advantage of using one's or two's complement to represent signed numbers is the same addition/subtraction hardware can be used for both signed and unsigned arithmetic. For eight bit unsigned numbers, the range is 0 to 255, and for signed numbers, the range is -127 to positive 128. For signed numbers, the high order bit indicates a negative number, while in 8-bit unsigned number, the high order bit indicates a value of 128 or more. So, if 100 is added to 100, the overflow bit is set indicating an error if the bit patter is considered signed, but is OK if the the number is considered unsigned.

9.3. Modify Listing 9.9 to copy the buffer from the end to the beginning by using register RCX as both the array index and loop counter. Hint: Use "R12,keymsg[8*RCX-8]" instead of "R12,keymsg[8*R15]"

```
57.              mov    RCX,MAXBUF      ; Buffer size in quad words
58. cpylp:       mov    R12,keymsg[8*RCX-8]
59.              mov    dismsg[8*RCX-8],R12
60.              loop   cpylp                    ; Continue until all copied.
```

9.2 Using the Scaled Index format, what instruction would implement ARRAY[I] = 6 if register EDX contained the value 6, ARRAY is an array of 32-bit integers, and register R15 represents the index I?

> MOV   ARRAY[4*R15],EDX

10.1 In Listing 10.2, why does the program output _*_* as the last line echoed?

The "Enter Key" places Carriage Return (hexadecimal 0D) and Line Feed (hexadecimal 0A) into the input buffer. When bit 5 (hexadecimal 20) is ORed with 0D0A, the result is 2D2A which represents the characters _*.

9.2 The packed arithmetic instructions do not set the carry and overflow flags. How could a program rather simply check for these conditions on every lane?

Do the addition twice: once in saturated mode and once not saturated. If the two results are identical, then no carries or overflow (if signed) occurred.

12.1 Convert the following real numbers into single precision IEEE 754 floating point and provide the answers in hexadecimal.

a. 128.0 is 43000000 in floating point
b. 9.25 is 41140000 in floating point
c. -9.25 is C1140000 in floating point
d. 0.03125 is 3D000000 in floating point
e. 128.03125 is 43000800 in floating point
f. 0.0 is 00000000 in floating point
g. -0.0 is 80000000 in floating point

12.2 Convert the following IEEE 754 floating point numbers back into real numbers in base 10.

a. 42A80000 is 84.0
b. C1A80000 is -21.0
c. 424C8000 is 51.125
d. BF100000 is -0.5625
e. 3DCCCCCD is 0.1

12.6 By examining Figure 12.1, what is the smallest absolute value non-zero normalized number?

Hint: Convert $1 \times 2^{1-127}$ to decimal.

12.10. Is getting that extra 1-bit of precision in the significant more important to the single precision, double precision, or half precision format numbers?

The half-precision floating point format is a 16-bit package containing a sign bit, five bits for the biased exponent, and ten bits for the significant. Note: Half-precision is only used for storage and is not supported for computation within IEEE 754 devices. That extra bit obtained by not taking up a bit-position for the most significant bit improves the resolution of the Half precision format the most.

- Half precision (significant is 10 bits): 1 in 2^{10}
- Single precision (significant is 23 bits): 1 in 2^{23}
- Double precision (significant is 52 bits): 1 in 2^{52}

The exclusive OR operation. Think back to your digital electronics days. How do you build a "half adder"?

12.11 Why will multiplying by 0.1 always result in a loss of precision in binary computers?

Base ten is not a multiple of base 2, like base 8 and base 16 are multiples. Some numbers like 0.1 cannot exactly be represented as a base two fraction for the same reason 1/3 is $0.333333..._{10}$.

49904705R00107

Made in the USA
Lexington, KY
25 August 2019